Praise from Parents

Raising children, especially teenage/young adults, is a daunting challenge. Each day is a new day and with it comes the positive aspirations for our children. We have three unique and very individual children, unique in their personalities, abilities and learning styles. As avid learners, we realized before the children were born that the most precious asset that we could instill in them was the love for learning. But as we all know, the best-laid plans aren't always what happens. What do you do as a parent when you see the special gifts of each child and the performance and feedback from school is disconnected from your reality? Am I biased as a parent? Yes! How do I go about "cracking the code"—the code that would be the key to relevant learning in the education system that they are in? How do I protect my children from the negative or perceived negative feedback that they might blatantly or subtly encounter in this process of discovery? How can we establish, and nurture, values, practices and skills that will result in our children having successful, meaningful, compassionate and prosperous lifestyles. Each of our three children has had their own life challenges and encounters from grades to self esteem, and lack of motivation for learning. In the predominant model of educating students, it is very clear that one size does not fit all. Through the Quantum Learning experience—the methods and techniques for teaching, the positive expectations, the learning environments they orchestrate, the life skills presented, and the personal and academic scenarios that they stage for each student—our children have become well rounded, happy, successful and contributing individuals. They have learned how they can get the most from any learning situation, and make the necessary adaptations to their learning styles and needs. Most importantly, there is a support system of peers who are willing to help with solutions and opportunities for growth. With SuperCamp as part of their life experience and tool box, each of our children has integrated the learning experiences as a part of their navigation system to living happy, meaningful and fulfilled lives. Today, each of our children is an honor student in college, working at careers that are meaningful and contributing to society.

—The O'Neills: Dwight, Merle, Jessica, Bucky and Amber,
Vista, California

Our daughter, Ashley, has always been a bright, intellectually curious person. However, with the emergence of her adolescence, Ashley began to show signs of distraction, disorganization, and lessening motivation with regard to her schoolwork. We became increasingly concerned that Ashley's considerable academic potential would decline to the point of seriously damaging the future quality of her life. After consulting with a variety of "educational experts" and using personal tutors, we eventually decided to send Ashley to a SuperCamp session at Stanford University. Ashley was not an enthusiastic participant in this decision. This was especially concerning in light of the fact that Ashley usually enjoyed a good intellectual challenge. Ashley fought her early experiences at SuperCamp, but shortly thereafter was enveloped by the extraordinarily positive and challenging environment. Upon the conclusion of this episode of SuperCamp, our family met Ashley at the airport. The young lady we greeted was strikingly different from the one we had sent to SuperCamp. She was calm, confident, reflective, focused, and demonstrated an uncharacteristic sense of personal responsibility. While pleased with the personal changes we observed, it was unlikely that they would be sustained in light of the relatively short experience of SuperCamp. Nonetheless, there were remarkable differences in our daughter. She made clear her intentions to return to SuperCamp the following year and potentially beyond. We enthusiastically embraced this ambition. The second SuperCamp experience had an even more profound impact upon Ashley. Her reading speed nearly quadrupled with increased comprehension. She developed a firm understanding of her learning style and how to approach instructional challenges in a format that best aligned with the manner in which she assimilates information. Furthermore, Ashley sharpened her academic focus and redeveloped a genuine enthusiasm for learning. She discovered a love for math and science, something for which there was no prior evidence. Ashley's academic performance accelerated through high school and continued to grow through her first year of college. Incidentally, she has achieved "junior" status after one year at college. Ashley loves college and is highly motivated. I credit Quantum Learning, and its amazing strategies, for refocusing and enhancing the learning potential of our daughter. It is not possible to fully articulate what you have done for our daughter and how this will affect the rest of her life.

I suppose the evidence of our view about this is summed up by the fact that our son will be attending his second SuperCamp this summer. We intend to send him every year until he graduates from high school. Thank you for all that you have done for our family.

—Robert J. Reid, Hobbs, New Mexico

Larry and I have sent all five of our kids to SuperCamp. Some of them have attended multiple times. None of them wanted to go as they thought it sounded dumb and they wouldn't be with their friends. All five of them returned declaring it was the best thing they had ever done. Out of their experience at SuperCamp all five kids stepped into leadership roles in their schools and began serving philanthropically in our community. Each of the kids learned the value of creating quality relationships especially with their family. They still practice the four-part apology. They communicate with the highest level of integrity and they do so in the most direct yet caring manner possible. The experience gained at SuperCamp provided the tools our kids needed to find themselves and to believe in themselves and to know in their heart of hearts they are good and worthy and loving. Oh, and by the way, they are all still in touch with friends they made at SuperCamp and some of those friendships span over ten years now.

—Kellie Lyle Hartstein, Scottsdale, Arizona

Each of our five children seems to use different tools that they learned at SuperCamp. It's difficult to pin down one or two specific benefits. For us as parents, the most powerful benefit for our kids is that SuperCamp helped us shatter the myth that children are victims of their circumstances. Each of our children caught a glimpse of their personal power during SuperCamp that has never left them. Our gratitude for that support truly runs deep.

—Larry Hartstein, Scottsdale, Arizona

Darren and I would have to say the most effective parenting tool we discovered while raising our two children was a wonderful, life-changing summer program called SuperCamp. Our son Austin was a nice young man exhibiting average effort in every aspect of his life. We knew that he had more in him and went about looking for an academic-like camp that was not a bunch of children with behavior or drug and alcohol issues. It was through the Young Presidents Organization that we learned about SuperCamp. We put out a national email to the membership asking if anyone knew of a camp like the one we described above. Five members called me back within a week and every single one of them had sent all of their children at least once, some up to three times. Austin agreed to go, teasing us the weeks leading up to camp that we were sending him to "nerd camp." When we went to pick him up at the end of the ten days, we were amazed at all the new friends he had made and how they all really seemed to care so much for one another. The graduation ceremony was amazing—I couldn't believe our son was participating in the exuberant manner he exhibited. Things had clearly changed in the last ten days. That school year he made As and got very involved in several school clubs. He was selected for the National Honor Society and for Senior Exec, an elite leadership group of students who are nominated by teachers and students. He made a lot of new friends as well. Midway through the school year he told us he needed to go back to SuperCamp to keep up his motivation and momentum. In his senior year, he made straight As all year, completed all of his college applications and was selected as "All Coronado Boy," the highest honor given to a senior student. The achievements, friendships, involvement, and leadership continue today in his college life. We ask, "How can he get any better?" And, he just does.

—Maria Woody, El Paso, Texas

SuperCamp gave our child the confidence to believe in herself without having to worry about what her peers thought of her. It equipped her with the skills to recognize that she had the strength to be her own person, and the ability to accomplish whatever she put her mind to. The tools she gained at SuperCamp have affected every area of her life, and she uses the skills daily. We are ever grateful, and highly recommend this program. SuperCamp works!

—Genette Waldman, Alpharetta, Georgia

SuperCamp has given my shy daughter, Devon, the courage and the self-confidence to attend camp this, her third year, as a part of the Leadership Team. Not a huge accomplishment by some parents' standards but to us, a Quantum leap. The growing self-confidence and self-empowerment she has been practicing since her first SuperCamp adventure, which, by the way, she needed to attend with a friend because she was too shy to go alone, has encouraged her to blossom into a wonderful young woman willing to face changes and challenges with a sense of self-assurance learned from the skills you teach at SuperCamp. It is so rewarding to see Devon embracing life and feeling good about her choices. I can't thank you enough for giving her the opportunity to achieve and excel.

—Rory Claire-Coppersmith, Pebble Beach, California

The 7 Biggest Teen Problems

And How To Turn Them Into Strengths

Complimentary Handbook www.TeenStrengths.com

The 7 Biggest Teen Problems
And How To Turn Them Into Strengths

An Inside Look at What Works with Teens
from a World Leader in Youth Achievement

By Bobbi DePorter

with SuperCamp Facilitators
Steve Arrowood, Chicka Elloy, Liesl Louw,
Amy Smith, Scott Wild

Published by Learning Forum Publications

Submit all requests for reprinting to:
Learning Forum Publications
1938 Avenida del Oro
Oceanside, CA 92056
(760) 722 0072

Cover and interior design: Bolger Creative
Contributors: The Writer's Lifeline, Patrick Wright, Sue Baechler
Editorial Support: Sheryl Freedman, Karen Borbolla, Genette Waldman, Sara Waldman, Sue Sinclair Pepe, Lori Goldsmith, Heidi Burke, Dee Conradie

Library of Congress Control Number: 2006930243

ISBN: 0-945525-39-7
ISBN-13: 978-0-945525-39-4

Printed in the United States of America

Dedication

To our wonderful, talented, and committed SuperCamp staff
who give so much of themselves to make a difference for children;
and to all the parents who believe what is possible
and entrust us with their amazing children.

Contents

Foreword

It may not seem fair, but there is no denying its truth: The actions that teenagers take today may shape their choices tomorrow. If teens make poor decisions now—for example, slacking off at school or avoiding social interactions—later on it will limit their options. Try as they might, however, parents cannot provide their children a magic formula for a happy and meaningful life. It just doesn't work that way. Throughout our lives we all face tough decisions and prickly dilemmas. The way we handle these challenges shapes who we are. But what if I told you that your teen didn't have to learn about life the hard way, slogging through trial and error for the next twenty years? Suppose I said there was a way he or she could learn the stuff that really makes a difference right now—on the threshold of adulthood?

There *is* a way. And you can help your teen find it. For the past twenty-five years, one camp has been making life-changing transformations happen for teens around the globe. SuperCamp has given more than 45,000 kids the chance to acquire years of hard-won experience in a dynamic program loaded with self-discovery and accelerated life skills. Bobbi DePorter and her business partners launched SuperCamp in 1981. Previously, Bobbi co-founded the Burklyn Business School, which blended the principles of accelerated learning and innovation to create a program that taught in six weeks what some business schools take two years to teach. The Burklyn students urged Bobbi and her associates to create a similar program for teens. The notion was compelling, for Bobbi and her colleagues observed that most schools relied on outdated "assembly-line" techniques that don't respect the individual learning styles of students and fail to engage young people as active participants in their own learning. They created SuperCamp to help kids reclaim the excitement of education.

For nearly 15 years I have been a professor in the university system. I guess by now I cease to be annoyed by the students who approach school like an obstacle course: hurdles they need to crawl under or jump over in order to achieve the grade they want. I make it my personal challenge each semester to inspire these students to love the process of learning. I tell them that they soon will enter a world of work that will value individuals who can apply intelligence and emotional tools to evolving environments. Memorizing a set of data or mastering a skill has a value, to be sure. In the 21st century, however, a law of diminishing returns immediately kicks in to depreciate the value of those personal assets. It jars my students—who obsess over the major of study they should choose—when I proclaim, "It really doesn't matter what you study, but it does matter immensely that you study with curiosity and passion." I latched onto Quantum Learning programs because it became obvious to me that, with notable exceptions, our school system is not preparing young people to learn effectively, discover their strengths, pursue goals, make decisions, solve problems and resolve conflicts.

SuperCamp prepares youth for creative, responsible citizenship in this 21st century with a dynamic program for learning personal and academic skills that last a lifetime. It mixes interactive theater with hands-on learning. Its mission is to empower young people to take ownership of their lives and reawaken their passion for learning. There's no other program like it. The Quantum Learning® method is taught by facilitators from around the world who have mastered Quantum Learning's strategies for content delivery, presentation skills, and creating model learning environments. The method engages students in any kind of content, reaches all learning styles, teaches kids how to learn, and provides a string of successes for forward momentum. These methods undergo constant, rigorous testing: what works stays; what doesn't work goes. Because of this purposeful evolution, SuperCamp gets results: 98% of teens who go keep using skills they learned at SuperCamp, 68% report an increase in motivation, and 73% improve their grades. Students report an 81% increase in confidence and an 84% rise in self-esteem. More importantly, SuperCamp grads discover their own greatness—their power to contribute their special kind of genius to the world.

Today, twenty-five years after its creation, SuperCamp's summer programs and school programs have impacted more than two million students and teachers—and have become sought-after methods for training future leaders of all ages. Bobbi DePorter's umbrella organization, the Quantum Learning Network, continues to expand and grow through camps and classrooms worldwide as she seeks new expressions for her boundless passion for learning.

Bobbi DePorter has a big vision for her SuperCamp. Yes, she is boosting student performance—*The Wall Street Journal* reports that SuperCamp "turns so-so students into academic achievers." Yet her more expansive dream is to set a new standard for learning and living that readies young people for a lifetime of meaningful achievement.

In this book you'll get an inside look into what happens within SuperCamp's programs. You'll find out why these simple shifts in attitude work, and you'll be able to adapt them to fit the lives of you and your teen.

David Batstone, Ph.D.

Dr. Batstone is *Worthwhile Magazine* Senior Editor; Professor, University of San Francisco; Founding Editorial Team, *Business 2.0*; Author, *Saving the Corporate Soul*

The 7 Biggest Teen Problems
And How To Turn Them Into Strengths

INTRODUCTION
45,000 Teen Success Stories and Counting

This book is not for parents who want things to stay the same between themselves and their children. It's for parents who are ready for something different— whether the changes they seek are great or small. This book is for the parents of all kids, straight-A to struggling, across all classes, cultures, and ethnicities.

It's the night before SuperCamp graduation. A hundred campers stand on a colorful stage ready to face an audience, their heads held high. Their eyes are bright. They can't believe how much they've changed in nine days. It's weird, but they like it! Triumphant music builds. One by one, they step forward.

"I am John Carlton. One thing I value in my life is integrity. I will show this by being honest with others. Tonight I take a stand for my greatness."

"I am Sara Goodson. One thing I value in my life is my family. I will show this by making time and sharing more of myself with them. Tonight I take a stand for my greatness."

When all the members of one team have completed their statements, the audience jumps to its feet in thunderous applause. The students on stage stand and take it all in.

Imagine your son or daughter on that stage. Alone in front of 100 other campers and a little nervous, but determined. Then—full of confidence—he or she looks straight ahead at the crowd and shares a deep personal value.

When young people find out what's inside them, they light up from within. They feel a shift in their energies and in their relationships: "Wow! I'm somebody special. I can be happy and take on anything in the world—just by being me!"

We know this is true because we've witnessed it repeatedly. We are the facilitators and leaders of SuperCamp. During the ten days of SuperCamp, teenagers come to see themselves in a positive way. They learn to connect with people. They get charged up about learning. They find out just how awesome they are.

All parents want their children to have an "I can" attitude—whether their children are excelling or struggling. Over the years many parents have told us that something seems to happen to their kids when they hit their teen years. In many cases, their children need a big boost in motivation, confidence, or academic achievement. In other cases, the loving happy child they knew has been replaced with a stranger. This new person may be sulky and withdrawn—or an emotional volcano. The smallest thing can set them off. They may disregard rules or start hanging out with friends who aren't good for them. Their grades tank. Their attitudes toward school go sour. They withdraw from friends and activities they once thought were cool. Parents often feel pushed away—just when it seems that they need to get closer.

When we talk about the problems teens face, we're not talking about serious emotional disorders or behavioral problems. We're talking about average young people. Even loving well-meaning parents see it happen. Some are scared. All of them are searching for better ways to help their kids through these challenges. They don't always know what to do.

You remember how great it was to watch your young child play at the playground. You felt wonder when your kid discovered a ladybug, learned to use a shovel, and interacted with others in the sandbox. You watched from a safe distance as your child explored the world independently. In the teenage years, you can no longer experience his or her life from the park bench. If you're like many parents of teens, you yearn for a view into your child's life, for a way to reconnect with your son or daughter the way you did during the early years.

Here's the good news—you still can. That disconnect that occurs between many parents and teens doesn't have to happen. You can find ways to keep the lines of communication open. It's possible for people to jump into their teen and adult years with confidence and joy. It's even possible to reverse that downward spiral into negativity once it's started. We see it every summer: Average students turn into academic achievers, and even young people who come in sullen and withdrawn go home open, loving, and energized!

What we do works.

Some teens, especially older ones, at first balk at the name "SuperCamp." The name doesn't capture the advanced, state-of-the-art nature of the program. We think of our program as a learning lab. At the end of each session, the staff gathers to evaluate, update, and retool. We identify what works and keep it; what doesn't work is revised or let go. We're different from most other programs because we're purposefully evolving.

Throughout the years parents have asked us to share what we've learned. They want to know what they can do to get a new view into their teens' lives. As we looked for ways to translate the SuperCamp process into a readable experience, we looked back at the differences between the way teens come to camp and the way they leave. We identified the most common difficulties we see them facing and boiled them down to seven main issues:

1. Troubled Relationships
2. Emotional Hurt
3. Negative Self-Image
4. Fear of Disruptive Change
5. Poor Grades
6. Lack of Focus
7. Low Motivation

The problems we see are the kinds of challenges everyone faces, young and old. Who hasn't had a poor self-image at one time or another? Who hasn't feared a major life change like parents divorcing, illness, or moving away from friends? These problems can derail our lives if we don't deal with them. When young people can't get on top of these problems, they miss out on social and academic development.

We've discovered that what's at the heart of each of these problems is a lack of self-awareness and a desire to be understood, combined with a need for social, thinking, and learning skills. At SuperCamp we've seen that when teens enter a uniquely positive environment of individual trust and acceptance, they begin to move beyond these problems. They feel safe to express themselves, explore who they are, and connect with one another. We use our 8 Keys of Excellence to provide a code that acts as a constant reference point for academic and personal excellence. Learning comes naturally in this environment, allowing teens to quickly adopt new academic strategies that will serve them for a lifetime.

---

8 KEYS OF EXCELLENCE

Live in **INTEGRITY**
Align your actions with your values

Acknowledge that **FAILURE LEADS TO SUCCESS**
View failures as information for learning

SPEAK WITH GOOD PURPOSE
Positive, honest and direct communication

Live in the Now—**THIS IS IT!**
Make the most of every moment

Affirm your **COMMITMENT**
Do whatever it takes

Take **OWNERSHIP**
Be accountable and responsible

Stay **FLEXIBLE**
Be willing to change to get your desired outcome

Keep your **BALANCE**
Live a fulfilled life by aligning your mind, body, and spirit

The 7 Biggest Teen Problems frames each of these seven challenges as teens experience them. We share what we've learned by seeing these problems from a teenager's point of view. You'll get a peek through the keyhole to see the transforming process teens go through. We'll let the campers themselves show you what works and why. You'll learn about the process they experience to increase personal accountability, develop a no-blame attitude, and take ownership for their needs, wants, and dreams. You'll see how they shift perspectives and change behaviors:

1. **Turning troubled relationships into confident communication**—articulating their ideas, thoughts, and feelings without second-guessing themselves.

2. **Turning emotional hurt into personal esteem**—taking charge of how events affect them, shrugging off rejections, turning failures into feedback, and keeping labels from sticking.

3. **Turning negative self-image into self-empowerment**—understanding their right to ask for what they want and recognizing the power of their special gifts, skills, and abilities.

4. **Turning fear of disruptive change into accepting change**—finding the self-determination to control the way they *think* about what happens to them.

5. **Turning poor grades into excelling in school**—taking responsibility for learning throughout their lives and creating environments that foster the joy of learning.

6. **Turning lack of focus into organized study strategies**—shifting attitudes and using concentration skills to get into a mindset of learning.

7. **Turning low motivation into goal achievement**—imagining success and following steps to reach goals both large and small.

SuperCamp is like a giant jigsaw puzzle of attitudes, expressions, and activities that together add up to something incredible. Each piece is presented on purpose and at the right time. We don't think of what we do as a series of strategies. We think of it as a process. It's more like ripples that build and crest like a wave. This book will give you a firsthand look at the way we move through that process. Take, adapt, and try anything we offer here. We leave it to you to make these experiences work for you and your teen, because we understand that every family is different. We don't have one solution that works for everyone. We encourage you to draw your own conclusions.

As a parent, think of this book as a new spot on the park bench—as a way to get a view into your teens' lives as they learn and grow.

The 7 Biggest Teen Problems is all about looking at young people from a different perspective: theirs. This perspective is foundational to SuperCamp and we call it our Prime Directive—theirs to ours and ours to theirs. Our goal is to help you understand your teen's unique point of view—from the outside looking in, then from the inside looking out. When parents and teens learn how to shift out of their old ways of thinking and reach into one another's worlds, everything changes.

It's a messy process. You have to dive in and experiment. You'll have to toss what doesn't work and tinker with what does. But if you keep working at integrating these ideas over time and, most importantly, if you keep the positive *intention*, the level of trust will increase between you and your teen.

As we said at the outset, this book is not for parents who want things to stay the same between themselves and their children. It's for parents who are ready for something different. At SuperCamp, we teach that your results only change when you change what you're doing.

It's more important than ever for parents to stay connected to their children. Today's world is filled with fast-moving information, choices, and decisions for teens. Parents who aren't aware of the changes in their sons' and daughters' lives will find it more and more difficult to understand them. It's as though they're on a speedway—and accelerating. If parents want to stay close to them as they grow, they have to keep up or they'll get left behind. Because SuperCamp is constantly evolving and changing with the times, we're in a unique position to help you get on the speedway and go along for the ride.

We believe that by sharing what we've learned about young people, we can help you facilitate a powerful transformation in your own teen.

Let's make it happen!

CHAPTER 1
Turning Troubled Relationships into Confident Communication

Andy expected to get everything he wanted—whenever he wanted it. Worst of all, his mom Robin realized, he never gave anything back.

Things came to a head one afternoon. Andy had used Robin's car three nights in a row and was planning to take it again. Robin said no. Andy demanded a good reason why she wouldn't let him use the car. Robin realized he played this game with everything, from borrowing the car to taking out the trash. He'd demand a reason. If he thought the reason she gave was good enough, he'd eventually give in. If he didn't, he'd refuse.

To Robin it often seemed as though Andy thought he was the center of the universe.

One of the reasons we love working with teens is that their relationship skills are works in progress. It's all a process of discovery: determining who they are in relation to the people in their world; sorting out the meaning of the interactions they have with others; and dealing with the flood of complex, conflicting, sometimes intense emotions that result. Teen relationships are kind of like a frontier—they're undiscovered territory. They face endless possibilities, because at this stage in their lives so many doors are opening to them.

Of course the frontiers of teen relationships can sometimes be tricky to navigate. There's bound to be some rocky ground to cover. If you have a teenager—or remember being one—you know how it can be. You set rules for her safety and she might scream, "Stop trying to run my life!" You try to explain that it's for her own good and you get back a sullen "what-ever." You get into what you think is a minor misunderstanding and she may sulk for a month.

And it isn't just with parents. Many teens' friendships spontaneously combust—sometimes over nothing. It's no different on the romance scene. The hottie they were all excited about last week might be a dweeb today. And the way they sometimes treat brothers and sisters—let's not even go there.

More frightening in some ways than the emotional firecrackers are the teens who go the opposite way. They won't look you in the eye. They answer your questions in monosyllables:

"How was your day, sweetie?"

"'kay."

"Did you get that report turned in?"

"Yeah."

"Anything exciting happen?"

"Nah."

"What else did you do today?"

"Nothin'." And off they go.

For some of them, it goes beyond a snippy comment or a case of the sulks. Some become hostile. They get into fights at school. Reports come home that they've been bullying others. They abandon their close friends and start hanging out with kids who are bad influences on them.

When parents see these kinds of changes in their teens, they want to take action. If their teens are hurting, they want to fix it. Unfortunately, it often seems that everything they do to help only makes it worse. They try to reach out, only to end up getting pushed away. Yet even during these stormy times parents generally are able to keep faith in their teens: "The wonderful person I know is still in there somewhere. At some point she'll resurface."

Of course the uncomfortable times aren't the whole story either. Even though it can sometimes be challenging to have a conversation with a teenager, these conversations can also be warm, open, candid, and trusting in a way that's refreshing to adults. Ask anybody what time in their life they made the deepest, closest friends. A lot of people look back on their teen years as the time when it was the easiest to open up to others.

These huge pendulum swings in teenager relationships make sense to us, because we recognize what they're going through. When their relationships are on rocky ground, it's a symptom of their struggle to figure out who they are. In a teen's mind, it's not that he's the center of the universe but that he's trying to find out in exactly what part of the universe he *does* belong. He has to focus on himself to find out where he fits.

From his point of view, the stormy moments can look particularly hopeless. Often, he's thinking, "Mom and Dad don't understand me. They have no idea what it's like to be me."

We've observed that, because they're so focused on their own identities, teens tend to take problems personally. They often think parents and others are saying that they *are* the problem. That's what ignites a lot of the emotional fireworks. It's rather like having a sore spot that you keep bumping against things. After a while it gets very tender and you become super-sensitive about protecting it. We've observed that teenagers' egos are especially tender because they're still forming—and teens don't yet have the self-protective emotional strength that grown-ups have developed.

Not only are they lacking the strength of grown-ups, many are also lacking basic communication tools. They've simply never been taught them. The main reason for that conversational disconnect is that often teens don't believe that anybody's really listening. They tell us that what they want more than anything else is to be heard and understood.

Teens and parents often come to their conversations from two different points of view. Parents get locked into speaking to their teens from the perspective of parents and teens from the perspective of teens. The moment one of them thinks their position is being challenged, they latch on even tighter to their own point of view.

No matter how loud the volume gets in these conversations, there's little real communication going on. Everybody's demanding to be heard; nobody's listening. But if you can't get someone to understand you, how strong is your relationship with him or her going to be?

We've observed that teenagers' trust is easily shattered, because the need to be understood is so huge—and so fragile. A teen says, "I can't go to school with this dorky haircut." All the parent has to do is reply, "You shouldn't worry so much about what your friends think," and poof—the teen's desire to continue the conversation is gone.

In this situation, it's not about the security and safety kind of trust, but the teens' ability to trust that their parents understand them. This kind of trust falls apart when communication breaks down. Once it's broken, how can it be rebuilt? How can the lines of communication be reopened?

Interactions look very different from where teens are standing. When we, as adults, have the experience of seeing from their perspectives, we create a whole new concept of how to approach them, talk to them, and help them. It transforms the way we interact with our children.

A Window Into a Teen's World

All loving parents strive to understand their teens. But sometimes parents aren't able to get a clear picture of their child's experiences because the information is filtered through their own adult points of view. They believe they must do this because it's part of their jobs as parents. Our number one goal is to get inside a teen's world.

Understanding teens is *what we do*. It's our life's work. We don't just focus on their perspectives; we *marinate* in them—day in, day out. And that obsession brings us an insight that we couldn't get any other way. It's mostly about becoming more aware of how we're relating to them.

Often, well-meaning parents try to solve problems for their teens before they fully understood their teen's perspectives. They speak from a grown-up's point of view instead of trying to see things through a teen's eyes. Program grad David Evans wrote, "So many parents are trying to turn their teens into things they're not, rather than trying to find out the things about their teens that are strong and true."

Our focus on hearing their perspective makes an impact. When they feel heard and understood, they're inspired to hear and understand others. A teen's whole concept of the world and his place in it shifts when he discovers what it looks like from someone else's point of view.

As it turns out, getting into another person's world is the fun part. Teens find it easier to do this when they interact with other people in a team atmosphere, where daily activities and traditions strengthen bonds between team members. At SuperCamp we weave team-building activities throughout our day. Every morning before breakfast, campers sing special team cheers for the facilitators. Music and rhythm are powerful aids to bonding. When our campers learn how great it feels to reach out and connect with others, they automatically begin to think further beyond themselves than they did before.

How Do Teens Know When It's Okay to Open Up?

A few days into camp, when the trust level is high, we divide campers into groups of four and ask them a series of questions about their inner dreams. We're very aware of their trust levels, and each question in the series moves a little deeper on the trust gradient. With each answer, students venture a little further out of their comfort zones. After they've spent a few minutes sharing, we ask them, "How does it feel to share those dreams with someone?"

Since the process of getting there is gradual, the teens often don't realize until this point how brave they're being. Their reaction is typically, "Wow! I'd never imagined I could do this!" Most of them say it feels great—scary, but great. Yet, just a few days earlier many of them could not have done it at all!

At this point they've spent several days in a place where they're accepted for who they are. They know that if they speak they'll be heard. It still makes them feel vulnerable to tell something so personal to people they just met days before. But it's a lot easier for them to step out of their comfort zones when they know they won't be laughed at, belittled, put down, or judged. In an environment of emotional safety, teens discover better ways to communicate. They can experiment and practice in such an environment because they know it's okay. Many of them have a space like this at home with their parents. Home has daily routines that are different from an organized program experience, but they share a common atmosphere of teamwork, trust, and a willingness to see things from another person's perspective.

I Know What I Want to Say—I Just Don't Know How to Say It

Good relationships are built on communication—and communication is a skill. In our ten-day interaction with campers, they learn and practice communication skills. They discover more about how to listen; get to know someone better; communicate what they want clearly and openly; apologize in a way that cleans up a hurtful situation; and express—constructively—their own feelings when they've been hurt.

In a master carpenter's toolbox there are many tools and each has its specific purpose. Similarly, a good communicator has many options and decides when and where to best use them. Here are some of the tools teens find most helpful.

The Gift of Being Heard

Often during SuperCamp, two facilitators act out a quick skit: Rachel comes up to her good friend Courtney. She's on the verge of tears.

"I just met Natalie and Colleen in the lunchroom and asked them to sit with me. They laughed at me and said no."

"Really?" says Courtney, absently twirling her hair. "What did you have for lunch?"

The conversation only goes downhill from there. When Rachel tells Courtney how rudely her two friends treated her, Courtney butts in with, "You think that's rude? You should've heard what Jamie said to me last weekend..." When Rachel says she's not sure how she's going to approach her two friends after this, Courtney says, "If I were you, I'd just tell those two little jerks to..." Rachel tries to tell Courtney how much Natalie and Colleen hurt her feelings, but Courtney says, "Don't worry. A month from now you'll barely remember it." And when Rachel tries to tell Courtney about her plan to confront the two of them next Friday after school, Courtney says, "Great. Wanna go to the mall afterward?"

After the skit the facilitator asks, "How does it feel to not be listened to?"

The teens have no problem answering this one. They've been there many times. It's frustrating. Painful. Makes you feel unimportant.

It helps to recognize that sometimes good communication skills are all about knowing what *not* to do—avoiding the things that sabotage a conversation. What's Courtney doing to mess up her conversation with Rachel—aside from twirling her hair, slumping over, and counting ceiling tiles?

Courtney's not listening very well because she's into the GABS: Grabbing the glory, Advising, Belittling, and Sidestepping.

Courtney's grabbing the glory by trying to outdo Rachel's story with one of her own—by saying things like, "I know exactly what you mean…but wait till you hear *my* story!" Doing this might make Rachel feel good for a minute, but what has Courtney just told her friend? "Your experience doesn't count. You have no reason to feel the way you do."

Courtney might think she's being a good friend by advising Rachel on what she thinks she ought to do. It's natural to want to help when someone comes to us with a problem. But probably all Rachel really wants is to be heard. Campers make a major communication break-through when they discover that most of the time people don't want someone to make it all better; they just want someone to care. Advice-giving, like glory-grabbing, steals attention from the speaker—with the result that the speaker doesn't feel respected.

A good rule of thumb for Courtney would be: If you're not being asked for advice, don't give it! It would be different if Courtney saw Rachel doing something dangerous like driving over the speed limit, or saw her developing a bad habit like smoking. In these situations you could even say she had an obligation to say something. But even then, since she's a friend rather than a parent, and the situation isn't immediately life-threatening, it's better if she asks Rachel's permission first.

When Courtney tells Rachel, "Don't get all worked up about a little thing like that; it's no big deal," her intentions are probably good. She doesn't want her friend to feel bad. But when she belittles her experience like this, it sounds to Rachel like she's just dismissed her feelings. Rachel won't be as likely to open up to Courtney in the future.

Everybody gets distracted sometimes. But when Courtney side-steps Rachel's story by focusing on unimportant details, she's unintentionally telling her friend that what she's saying isn't worthy of her full attention. It can also be hard on teens when parents side-step. What seems like nothing to the parent may be important to the teen. There's also more at stake for them than the subject of conversation. When adults don't pay attention to what they're saying, teens take it personally. "You don't take what I'm saying seriously" often translates in their minds to, "You don't take *me* seriously."

By now, teens have a pretty good picture of what *not* listening looks like. Now let's turn it around. Let's say it's a week later and Rachel has just had another run-in with Natalie and Colleen. Courtney's been working on her communication skills lately, so this time when her friend talks to her, Courtney uses her EARS: Expression, Attentiveness, and Restatement.

When Rachel tells Courtney about the unkind things Natalie and Colleen said about the way her backside looks in her new jeans, Courtney shows Rachel she's listening by her expressions: She nods and makes eye contact. While Rachel tells the whole story of this latest encounter, Courtney stays attentive: She leans forward and keeps her hands still. And when Rachel is finished with her story, Courtney says, "And you said they did all this right in front of the principal?" Because Courtney has just restated important parts of the story, Rachel *knows* she got it this time.

The magical thing about using your EARS is that it actually turns the person talking into a better speaker. Campers *experience* the fact that people communicate better when the person they're talking to is really listening. It seems like common sense, but it's an easy thing for people to miss until they've deliberately lived it. They become more acutely aware of "all the things I never learned because I wasn't really listening."

How does it feel to be heard? Like somebody cares. Many teens don't realize that in most conversations, showing they care is the best thing they can do. Campers get a huge boost to their communication abilities when they really *get it* that this is what our friends and family come to us for most of the time—not for us to fix their problems or make it all better, but just to be heard. It can be an awesome experience for parents when a son or daughter opens up and shares something deep and personal he or she has never talked about before. Sometimes one heart-to-heart conversation can rekindle the relationship between parents and teens.

What if you made the time to sit down with your child once a week without distractions and really talked? What if you asked questions that didn't yield yes-or-no answers: What's your biggest challenge in school? Who are your closest friends right now?

Making Connections

Imagine you know a really sweet but somewhat introverted teen, Derek, who's just moved to a new town. Derek wants to make friends, so he goes to as many parties as he can. But once he's there, Derek finds himself tongue-tied. He's in a room full of cool people but can't start a conversation with any of them. People start to refer to him as "that standoffish guy." Every once in a while, a girl looks at him and smirks, "What's his problem?"

Is he shy? Maybe. But probably what's keeping Derek from making new friends is simply not knowing *how* to get to know somebody. Nobody ever taught him what to say to get a conversation going.

We've observed that many teens—and a pretty large number of grownups—have never been taught basic techniques for getting to know other people. They're not sure what personal information to volunteer, and they don't know what to ask someone in casual conversation. Finding common ground is hit or miss.

There are all kinds of ways for teens to find common ground—most of them take the form of quick-and-easy connections that pave the way for the more meaningful ones. Teens can develop the ability to find common ground with people in almost any circumstance, but it's a lot easier for them to learn how to do this when it's modeled for them.

When we partner campers for pair-and-share activities, we'll say, "Find somebody who has the same number of siblings as you." Or who has the same number of doors in their bedroom. Or who would pick the same toppings on a pizza. During various exercises, they share bits of themselves: scariest moments, favorite places. But one of the most powerful things we do to forge connections is the Affinity Exercise. Here's how it goes:

Ask your conversation partner to respond to these three statements: "Tell me something I don't know about you." "Tell me something you like about me." And, "Tell me something we have in common or agree on."

No matter how their partner responds, they don't say anything except "thank you" after each answer. When players know that the response will just be "thank you," without judgment or commentary, they feel freer to express themselves.

Teens ask their partners all three questions a total of three times. Then they switch. Why three times? The first two times, players may feel awkward and embarrassed, so they answer with superficial stuff: "I bet you didn't know I washed my car this weekend." Often something happens on the third time through—that's when some of the most meaningful answers come out. Teens say that even though it's scary, sharing personal thoughts with somebody who's *really listening* feels great!

Let's say Derek, the shy new kid, practices the Affinity Exercise at home a few times with his parents. He finds out that his dad used to fly crop dusters in college and that he and his mom share a desire to visit Germany's Black Forest someday. He also finds out that both his parents love the crazy stories he tells his little sister at bedtime.

Family members don't have to adhere to the only-say-thank-you rule when they're using the exercise to generate conversation because some of the best family conversations can come out of the responses to their questions. But if they stick to the three-times rule they'll probably be amazed at the stuff that's revealed the third time around!

So with some practice under his belt, Derek goes to the next party and starts up a conversation with a girl he knows a little from trigonometry class. When he asks her a question that shows he's interested in who she is, she laughs nervously, but she's flattered. Their conversation soon becomes so animated that it attracts other people. And the ice is broken.

When the Talk Changes, the Relationship Changes

A well-stocked communication toolbox contains speaking tools alongside the ones for listening. One of the 8 Keys of Excellence is called Speak with Good Purpose, which is all about making sure you don't speak unless the intent is positive. This key isn't a foreign concept to our campers; they've learned the basics of it at home—which is the reason they latch on to it so easily during our programs.

You can Speak with Good Purpose even if you're giving feedback in areas where people could benefit from improvement. If a friend is practicing for a vocal solo in a concert, you can tell her that her high notes sound flat—that would still be speaking with good purpose, even though it might sound negative. The *intent* is positive: to help your friend give the best performance possible.

Nobody speaks with good purpose 100% of the time, but it's the kind of skill that gets stronger the more you make yourself aware of it.

We've seen that relationships can get better when the patterns of communication change. When two people make a commitment to Speak with Good Purpose, the energy of their interaction shifts. Just changing the way one person talks to another can make a significant difference in their relationship.

One parent decided to give up berating her son about his poor study habits and his messy room. For one month she would only comment on positive things. Within a couple of weeks, she noticed that her son spent more time in the kitchen after school, just hanging out and talking about his day. That change alone, she reported, made the new habit worthwhile.

No Tricks or Traps When You Talk to Me

"What are you doing Friday night?"

Facilitators ask this question to a roomful of campers. To the one who responds, "I'm busy," the facilitator says, "Well, I have two tickets to *Star Wars*. But that's okay; you're busy." He continues asking around the room until a teen says, "Nothing." Then the facilitator replies, "Great! Because I have these two tickets to *Star Wars*...and I'd love it if you'd babysit so my date and I can go!"

Or the alternative: The facilitator goes around the room asking, "What do you think of Britney Spears?"—or any other famous person teens can relate to. To the teens who say she's great, the facilitator says, "You really like her? Wow! She's the geekiest person I ever saw. You must be weird, too." To a negative response, the facilitator says, "How could you not like her? She's like a sister to me!"

Everyone's been in conversations like these. When we ask how they felt about this kind of communication—invisible communication—the teens usually toss out words like trapped, manipulated, and defensive. They say that this kind of talk makes them distrust the other person.

Like all relationship skills, visible communication takes practice. If teens find themselves falling into the same old lines, they know how to fix it. Instead of just asking, "Are you free on Saturday night?" they can do a quick save and add "...to help me with my English paper?" When they're on the receiving end of an invisible communication, they can respond with, "Why are you asking?" or "Tell me more."

Teenagers can sometimes use a little help understanding that the conversation turns out a lot better when they let people know up front what the communication is about. One of the best ways to get what you want is to say it—not in a pushy or demanding way, but simply, "Here's what I want."

All Stressed Up and Nowhere to Go: Conflict Resolution Skills Ease the Tension

Almost every parent and teen has been through highly charged conversations in which feelings get hurt and emotions get out of control. We know that even adults struggle with conflict resolution. Add the explosiveness of teen emotions to that mix and it's no wonder they have trouble expressing hurt feelings in positive ways. Teens find it extremely helpful when they're able to express painful topics in a way that doesn't make the conversation more volatile.

Picture this: Two friends pass one another in the hall. One says, "Hi!" and the other says nothing.

Now it's the next day and the two friends pass in the hall again. This time, the friend who said, "Hi!" stops the other friend and says, "Is something wrong with you? You don't like me anymore or what?" The other person gets confused and defensive.

Now let's run through it again. This time, the day after the friend doesn't say "Hi!" back, the other friend says, "Hi! Do you have a minute? Listen, yesterday I passed you in the hallway. I said hi and you didn't respond. I thought either you didn't hear me or you were deliberately ignoring me. I felt really bad and confused. Even if your mind is on something else, my desire is for you to say hi so I know you're not mad at me."

What's the difference between these two scenarios? In the second, the friend who felt ignored Opened The Front Door.

Open The Front Door, or OTFD, stands for Observation, Thought, Feeling, and Desire. Its goal is to air feelings in a clear and positive way while focusing on a solution to the problem. When we Open The Front Door instead of laying blame and passing judgment, the conversation stays on the issue, not on the person.

It helps teens to open an emotionally painful subject with a simple observation, something anybody could comprehend with their senses: "I noticed you canceled our plans to go to the movies this weekend. This is the third time you've made plans with me and then canceled them at the last minute." This process allows a teen to put himself into the picture by saying what he thinks about the observation: "I think you only want to do stuff with me when there's nothing better to do." Next comes the painful part, the feelings. However, since the problem has been set up in a simple, factual, non-judgmental way, the teen may find it easier to express the way the situation makes him feel: "I feel hurt because you're not spending time with me when you said you would. And I feel annoyed because if I'd known you were going to cancel, I could've made plans with other friends." Finally, the teen can add the really empowering part, the desire—what he wants the friend to do differently: "From now on, I'd like it if you'd make plans with me only when you intend to keep them."

OTFD works because it clears the situation of doubt and hidden agendas. Even if the person is still upset and angry, the technique brings a level of calmness to the situation. When you Open The Front Door, what you see is what you get. The problem is laid out for all to see. It's a lot easier to focus on a solution when everybody involved is clear about the problem.

Teens learn that desire is the most important part of this process— that they have the best chance of receiving what they want in life if they *understand* what they want.

After they get a feel for the steps to Open The Front Door, teens pair off and practice it in different scenarios: The friend who was an hour late to a meeting. The person who rolled his eyes at something you said. The friend who didn't listen when you were telling her something important. These are the kind of situations they get into just about every day. They also discover that they can use OTFD to talk to a friend who seems to have a problem: "I like hanging out with you and if nothing's up, that's great. If there is anything, I'd like us to get it cleared up. Can you tell me what happened?"

OTFD may feel funny at first, and it doesn't guarantee success every time. But just knowing they have a tool that helps them get feelings across in a non-accusatory way helps boost teens' confidence in social situations. And simply going into conversations with more confidence can make a big difference.

It helps a lot for teens to see firsthand how OTFD makes a difference in conversation. The SuperCamp environment gives them the chance to practice it and get comfortable with it in a place where they're supported. It's okay if they don't get it perfect the first few times.

Teens sometimes teach their parents about OTFD. Parents find it valuable in a number of situations. In addition to being a great conflict-resolution tool, it's also a terrific way for parents to acknowledge the good things their kids do. Instead of saying, "I'm proud of you for getting an A," a parent could say, "I saw you putting a lot of effort into writing a good report (observation) and I thought you really cared about doing a good job (thought). It made me feel really proud (feeling). I hope you feel great about yourself for accomplishing this (desire)."

Teens get a confidence boost from OTFD because it gives them a way to resolve hurt feelings. But they're also aware that sometimes *they're* the ones doing the hurting. Even if their intention is to Speak With Good Purpose, sometimes they forget or get mad and say something hurtful. At times like these it helps to have a way to clean up the damage so that they and the person they've hurt can feel better.

A teen is fiddling with a broken iPod when his friend walks in.

"Hey! I didn't know you had an iPod like mine!"

"Actually, I don't. This is yours. I kind of borrowed it without asking, and then I kind of broke it. Sorry."

Most teens have been in this kind of situation. How does it feel? Even though the friend said, "Sorry," they'd still be angry.

Since we all screw up sometimes, it helps us to be able to apologize in a way that doesn't leave hard feelings—and in a way that has more sincerity than a lame "sorry." The teen in this skit can show his friend that he's taking responsibility for what he did and that he's ready to take whatever action is necessary to make it right.

A really great apology takes four steps: acknowledge, apologize, make it right, and recommit. First, the friend can acknowledge what he did wrong: "I know that I borrowed your iPod without permission." Next, he can apologize and acknowledge the cost of what he did: "I apologize for invading your privacy, and I realize you may have lost your trust in me." Then, to bring things back to a baseline of okay, he can offer to repair the damage: "I want to make it up to you. In three months I can save up enough to buy you a new iPod." But now that he's possibly wrecked his friend's trust, he realizes it would be a good idea to do something to earn it back. He can make a commitment to behave differently in the future: "From now on, I promise to ask before I borrow anything from you."

If the teen who broke the iPod apologizes this way, there's a good chance that the iPod will be the only thing that's broken; the friendship will stay intact. This kind of apology helps teens focus on positive action—on making it right again—at a time when things might otherwise degenerate into a hurtful argument. It's hard for the wronged person to stay angry when he gets a heartfelt apology and a commitment to different behavior in the future.

This kind of apology can be just as effective for long-term, ongoing hurts as it is for one-time incidents. Once we had a brother and sister attend our program at Stanford. When we were practicing apologies, the brother spoke up before all the other teens and told his sister, "I know I'm not always nice to you. I know how much it must hurt you. What can I do to make it better?"

The sister stared at him for a minute. The other campers held their breaths. Were they about to witness a family fight?

Then, with tears coursing down her cheeks, she said, "Give me a hug. Just knowing that you know makes it better."

Imagine how it would feel to hear your kids apologize in this way. You might feel an immediate sense of peace, and confidence in your teen. And whatever the issue, it seems to disappear in the genuine apology coming from your child.

This kind of apology isn't for frivolous things that carry no emotional power. It's for situations that have caused hard feelings. It's important for teens to understand this because using it in a situation that doesn't call for it makes it look as though they're over-reacting.

Once at graduation, a boy stood up and addressed his father in front of a hundred grads and parents. He said, "I didn't want to come to SuperCamp. In fact, for a time I flat out refused. I yelled at my dad and told him I hated him. Dad, would you please stand up." Dad stood with his arms crossed over his chest, ready for whatever his son was going to throw at him. "Dad, I acknowledge that I gave you a really hard time about sending me to SuperCamp. I apologize. I was wrong. This was the best experience of my life. I want to know what I can do to make up for the hard time I gave you. I commit to being more open to what you say in the future."

The dad slowly dropped his arms. His eyes started to tear. They walked toward each other and, in front of everyone, hugged. The entire room was in tears.

A Walk in Mom and Dad's Shoes

It's evening, an hour or two after dinner. Campers have been going full-throttle since 7:00 a.m. They file in with stimulated minds and open hearts. The lighting is subdued, the room quiet. Soft music plays: songs that speak of the love between parents and children. Quietly, the teens take a seat on the floor, settling into the mood.

Tonight, teens journey deep into the most important relationship in their lives, the one they've been forging since birth: their bond with their parents or caregivers.

As the parent talk begins, the teens are asked to rate their relationship with their parents on a scale of one to four, from fair to great. Next, we make two lists: What's Right about My Parents, What's Not Right about My Parents. For "Right," teens usually list things like "spend time with me, help with homework, listen." Under "Not Right," it's things like "dress stupid, try to impress my friends, control my life, compare me to my brother/sister." During this exercise, they begin to realize that their relationship with their parents is a mixed bag. It's not all bad, even though some might have come to think of it that way.

Next, they become their parents. We ask them to close their eyes, transport themselves into their parents' bodies, and look at themselves from their parents' point of view. Now we ask them to list What's Right and What's Not Right about *themselves*. This exercise is an eye-opener for many teens—especially when they compare the two lists and realize that several of the items on both lists are the same. Their parents probably aren't crazy about the way they dress either.

And then they get it: "Wow! My parents want the same thing I do!"

A grad, Anna, wrote what she discovered about her relationship with her parents: "...I often feel frustrated with my dad. He tends to think that I need to be sheltered so that I won't end up making mistakes...He also opposes my open-minded self mainly because he thinks he can no longer control how I manage my life. I felt as if I was losing my genuine self under the guidance of my dad's stern personality. Truthfully, I didn't have any goals or ambitions to look forward to...I retraced my history with my parents and finally understood that I never gave them the chance to know who I am. I've always fought with them, explaining pieces of my resentment without telling them the whole problem. It was partly my fault for not making an effort to communicate with them. I forget that they are always there for me."

While that awakening is still tingling in their minds, campers go a step deeper. They close their eyes again. Then we tell them a story—*their* story:

> Picture your parents way back before you were born. Imagine how they looked when they were just beginning: happy, excited, getting to know each other. Then they found out you were on your way. They were thrilled. They bought clothes for you. They planned your room. They were nervous—they wanted to do everything right for you. Then you were born. They held you, took you home, and showed you off. You were helpless and they took care of you. They watched you grow. They let go of your hand on the first day of school. They answered your questions and took you to your practices. But then something happened: You became a teenager. Now their encouragement felt like nagging; being there for you felt controlling. They were confused. They were just doing the same things they'd always been doing but now you didn't like it anymore. Now visualize your parents as they are today. They still want to do the best they can for you because they love you. Can you forgive them for all the mistakes they made in bringing you up?

Now the campers open their eyes. They discover that the staff has placed paper and pens all around the room. By this point in the parent talk, many are burning with unexpressed emotions. Some of them even rush off to the phone during breaks and call home. At this point we give them a chance to write a letter to their parents. They can write whatever they want to communicate. The letter is private. They can send it or not.

The experience wraps for the evening as campers complete this statement: "One thing I can do to accept my parents for who they are..." putting their new shift in attitude into action.

A SuperCamp mom wrote of the night her son came home from camp: "...As we approached the house, Brian asked if we could have a 'serious' talk when we got home...We talked until 1:00 A.M. about his life and experiences and how different events have affected him...He thanked us many times during the conversation for 'hanging in there with him' and loving him despite his emotional withdrawal...This was a major turning point in his life."

Many teens and parents write us that the parent talk, more than anything else they experienced in our program, changed their lives.

CHAPTER 2

Turning Emotional Hurt into Personal Esteem

DeeDee's son came home from school in a rage. He'd been kicked off the swim team for bad grades. He said when he went to practice that afternoon, the principal berated him loudly in front of all his teammates and kicked him off the team right there and then.

DeeDee grabbed her son's report card and a calculator to see whether he really had missed the cut-off point. She did the math four times and came up with the same number—a number above the minimum average for being on the team.

She confronted school officials. They quietly let her son back on the team and never apologized for the incident. But the damage was done. Her bright, cheerful, questioning son had become sullen, sad, and withdrawn.

In a teen's world, failure and rejection happen practically every day. For twenty-five years we've been listening to teens talk about times they've been rejected, labeled, judged, or dismissed. These painful moments can change them, diminish them, and destroy their self-confidence.

Parents like DeeDee watch their sons and daughters go through failures and rejections that take away some of their enthusiasm for life. These parents know that emotional hurt is a normal part of life, but they wish they could help them learn how to keep failures and disappointments from derailing their dreams.

One time a teen came to us whose whole way of acting and dressing seemed to say "I don't fit in." He wore all black, had long black hair, and his taste in music was—let's just say unusual. Some of the other campers stared at him. He felt like an outsider. Finally, it became unbearable for him and he asked to leave. We talked to him for a long time—we wanted him to stay. But his mind was made up. He wanted out.

That night during one of the group shares, another camper stood up and talked about his own feelings of rejection and being left out. He apologized to the teen in black for the assumptions he and some of the other students had made about him. Then he asked him to stay: "The group needs you, man."

It was pretty emotional after that. The teen in black stayed. And in the end he was glad he did.

What made it possible for him to overcome that rejection? Knowing that somebody saw past the Gothic clothes and the different music and valued him for who he really was.

We've learned from teens that failures, labeling, and rejection affect them so much because they're still working out who they are—and they're relying on external cues to tell them: "I flunked AP calculus; I'll never make it in college." "Derek called me a nerd. I must be a nerd." "Jaime wouldn't go out with me. I'll never get a date."

Nobody needs to tell them that rejection and failure are part of life. They've lived it. And they know there's no way to avoid it. But what they might not know is that there's a way to keep these experiences from getting in the way of their success.

Shrink to Fit

"What are some of the labels you've been given?"

Dumb blonde. Pot head. Wanna-be. Loser. Ditz. Band geek. Drama queen. The labels don't even change all that much through the years. Some of them are the same ones their parents endured.

In our program, campers spend a large chunk of a day working with the labels they've been given—and the labels they've put on others. Teenagers get labeled every day, just as adults do. We label one another without thinking anything of it. One of our facilitators came in with coffee one morning and someone said, "Are you a Starbucks girl?" Some of the labels people give us are accurate; some aren't.

A label isn't inherently bad or good. It just is. It's how we identify, define, and categorize in order to decide how to react to a situation. People label us so they can decide how to deal with us. It's only when we let those labels stick to us and define us that they become problems.

As long as we understand that we're not the label and the label is not us, we're fine. But since teens are still working on their sense of self, it's more difficult for them to distinguish between their labels and their true selves. And sometimes it's easier for them to accept the labels other people stick on them than to be exposed for who they are.

When they start to define themselves by the labels other people give them, they volunteer for powerlessness. They let something on the outside determine their inside. No label can possibly capture all the complexities and possibilities of a person. So when teens see themselves as their labels, it's as if they shrink to fit. They begin to see who they are and what they're capable of within the confines of that label—a label somebody else stuck on them!

You Don't Have to Reject Me—I'll Do It Myself

"I was shy and unapproachable," shared a camper by the name of Laci. "I didn't like who I was. I didn't like my awkward conversation attempts. I didn't like my fear of other people's opinions about me." Laci went on to tell the group that her fear of rejection caused her to shy away from talking to people. Rejection can be so hurtful for teens that they'll do anything to avoid it—and as a result, they miss out on a lot of great opportunities.

Teens want very much to know they're okay. Rejection seems to them like a personal indictment. It's as though they're asking the world, "Can you accept me as I am?" and whenever a person or group rejects them, it seems to them that the world has just answered no.

When they're afraid to risk rejection, they avoid situations that might result in acceptance. Imagine a teen starts to make friends with a couple of girls at her school. But she begins to realize that these particular girls are considered popular at her school, and she's afraid they'll reject her because they only hang with other girls in the "in" crowd. She begins to avoid them. The girls get the impression *she* doesn't like *them*, so they stop making an effort to talk to her. In cases like these, fear of rejection leads to a kind of self-fulfilling prophecy.

That Failure Is Me

Teens, feeling their way toward self-identity, often internalize their failures. Rather than saying, "I failed," they might make it a part of themselves: "I'm a failure." A bad grade on an algebra test means "I'm no good at math." Not making the callback list for the school play means "I stink at acting." They discourage themselves from trying again because they're afraid to risk another failure.

With any failure, there's a big difference between the way it looks on the outside and the way it affects a teen on the inside. The outside effect is usually pretty small—a one-time occurrence, a flashbulb in time: "My girlfriend dumped me." "I flunked English." "I didn't make the team." But what happens inside can be devastating—a ripple that keeps on expanding. "Girls think I'm a dork." "I'm too stupid to handle college." "I'll never be an athlete."

If we rewind the tape of their lives fifteen years or so, we go back to a time when they weren't afraid to fail. When they were toddlers, the world was their laboratory and failure was part of the experiment. It was how they learned what did and didn't work. They didn't learn to internalize until they became teenagers and got their egos invested in the outcome. Now their experiments are less about "how does the world work?" and more about "how do *I* fit into it?" They look at everything that happens to them for clues about who they are. That's why it's so tough for teens to detach their egos from their failures. That's why they tend to turn "I failed" into "I'm a failure."

I Can Take a Painful Event and Flip It

What do teens' experiences of labeling, rejection, and failure have in common? They're all external events that they tend to internalize. They take an event and make it part of their identity. The pain isn't in the event itself; it's in how they're thinking about it.

And that's the one thing they can do something about.

As they work through their experiences with these painful events, teens come to the realization that even though they can't control what happens to them or what people think of them, they *can* control *how they think about it.*

At that moment something incredible happens. They discover that no matter what a given moment brings, they can turn it into something great: "This is my chance. I have an opportunity to take something painful and flip it."

Taking charge of the way they think about an incident comes more naturally once they're able to separate themselves from the situation: "I am not the thing that's happening. I exist separately from this event." Once they shift from being the passive victims of external events to taking charge of how the events will affect them, it's as though a light goes on inside them. It's what makes it possible for teens to shrug off rejections, turn failures into feedback, and keep labels from sticking.

That Label Isn't Me

On night six of SuperCamp, teens have a chance to go deep into the experience of being labeled. They talk about the labels people have given them—especially the ones they've hung onto. They explore the reasons they chose to hang onto those labels—are they useful in some way? Do they cover up something? What has it cost them to use these labels?

"How congruent is your label with your true self? How do you want to present yourself now—as your label, or as your true self?" Many campers have an "Aha!" moment the first time they consciously separate themselves from their labels. All of a sudden they realize they have the power to choose! They can let a label stick, or they can let it go.

One time a teen who wore the label of "obnoxious kid" came to our program. He acted out this label everywhere he went, roaming the fringes of the group and being disruptive. The others made it clear that they didn't like his behavior, but they still accepted him. He came to realize that he wasn't his behavior. Toward the end of camp, he sat in the middle of the group instead of acting up on the fringes. He discovered he liked being seen for who he was. He still wasn't the best-behaved, but a shift had occurred in the way he interacted with people. He had dropped the label of obnoxious cut-up because he felt accepted for who he was.

When teens are able to accept themselves for who they are, they discover their own power to refuse labels. Sometimes campers come up to us at the end of the labeling process and say, "Why didn't anybody *tell* me I didn't have to live up to these labels?" It had never occurred to them!

We don't have the power to stop people from slapping labels on us. But we have the power to choose not to let them stick. We don't have to *be* the labels.

During the labeling process, campers discover how to escape the negative impact of labels. They also learn to let go of labeling others. At one point, they gather into circles—they know little or nothing about the people in their circles at this point. The facilitator says, "Point to the person in your circle who you think is most likely to spill food on themselves." Then it's the person most likely to like rap music, get married at a young age, have the most friends, get bad grades, and so on.

"Did you agree 100% with the other opinions you saw in the circle?"

They recognize that impressions vary a lot from person to person. They're arbitrary.

They all know from experience what it's like to be judged incorrectly. They know how it feels to have opinions formed about them. When they explore this idea, they discover that they too sometimes make assumptions about people based on impartial, or even no, information.

A camper named Jenn wrote that the labeling process caused her to stop and think. She realized that labeling may seem like harmless fun, but it could put a long-lasting judgment on the person being labeled. She realized that she wanted to respect people more and stop labeling.

"What could you do instead of labeling someone?"

Once they have come to this deep understanding of the impact of labeling—on themselves and others—teens are invested in the answer to this question.

Their response: "Get to know the person for who they really are."

Teens are empowered when they recognize that labels and judgments stick to people only as long as we let them. When they have a strong sense of who they really are, they can let go of labels.

I Don't Have to Take It!

Imagine this. One hundred teens are sitting in a room. An adult dressed in black goes around to each person and says, "I reject you because you have a geeky name. I reject you because you're five-foot-two. I reject you because you ride a bicycle instead of driving a car." To make it tangible, the rejecter even hands out a rejection slip to go with the rejections.

Some teens accept the slip meekly. Others get giggly. Some of them make a game out of it and call the rejecter over to give them their rejections. Then the reaction builds. Rejection upon rejection, the tension piles up. Then we hit a breaking point. Finally, someone refuses the paper—or hands it back: "I am *not* that." They will take no more rejection.

When this happens, the energy in the room shifts. Everybody feels it. They stop accepting the rejections that are coming their way. Then the magic happens. They realize *they don't have to take it!*

Once we had a camper who attended on a scholarship. His mother had been in jail and he hadn't had a permanent father figure in his life. He was the first one to refuse another rejection. But he told us afterward that *he* was the one who was the rejecter in his school. He went around putting everyone down. That night he decided he didn't want to do that anymore.

It helps to separate the person from the behavior; to recognize that there are all kinds of reasons for people to reject others. Most of them have little to do with the person they're rejecting. Campers can learn to deflect every negative comment out of habit. They can get used to assuming it's something going on with the rejecter instead of something about them: "Wow, she really got up on the wrong side of the bed today." Or, "Maybe somebody's being mean to him." Or, "Maybe he's under a lot of stress because his dog died." Making it about them makes just as much sense as assuming it's about us—and it's a lot less damaging to our sense of self.

Failure: My Ticket to Success

Failure Leads to Success. Campers probably mention this Key of Excellence in their letters to us more than any other. It's a life-changer. The message of this key is straightforward: Success is not about not failing; it's about learning from failures until you succeed. Each time you go for something and fail, you've gained a valuable piece of information. You now know one more thing about what it takes to succeed. Instead of seeing failure as proof of our inadequacy, we can choose to see it as a necessary ingredient in our success.

It feels fantastic to discover that we have that power. We love watching teens light up when they realize the power they have over their own lives. Their posture changes, their faces change. You can hear it in their voices. They radiate it.

They talk about this key a lot when they're exploring rejection, labeling, and failures because it gives them the power to turn around a painful event. When something emotionally hurtful happens, they can decide whether to soak in their misery or mine the experience for news they can use.

As they role-play different scenarios they discover endless uses for this key. You got kicked off the soccer team for bad grades? Time to work out a strategy to raise those grades. Got turned down for a date? Go get some pointers from your friend the "hottie magnet." Didn't make callbacks for the school play? You can track down the director and find out what you can work on between now and the next audition.

Teens can turn their response to failure into a habit: "Whenever things don't turn out the way I planned, I look for the action most likely to give me different results next time and I throw myself into it with all I've got."

Nothing's Gonna Stop Me from Being Me

If failure, rejection, and labels hurt because teens think they *are* those things, then the flip side goes like this: "I know who I am. I'm not that failure. I'm not that label. I don't have to take that rejection."

Teens discover that when their sense of self is strong, it's easier to resist blaming themselves when things go wrong. They're better able to maintain an identity separate from the labels others try to give them. They're able to keep their balance in the face of rejection and recognize failure as an opportunity for improvement.

The direction of one grad's life changed when she began to accept herself for who she truly was: "Instead of living with a negative attitude where I believed that everyone was out to get me, I realized I was the one with the power. I began to feel really good about myself...Up to this point, I had been very shy and afraid to connect with people...with every experience and every choice now, I say to myself, 'This is how I want to live my life...'"

CHAPTER 3
Turning Negative Self-Image
into Self-Empowerment

In seventh grade, Maddie's English teacher told her she was stupid. Instead of trying to understand Maddie's dyslexia, the teacher would comment about her horrible spelling in front of the class. Even though Maddie qualified for a gifted-level English class, the teacher kept insinuating that she didn't belong. At the end of the semester, the teacher gave her a D, the lowest grade she'd ever gotten.

The blow to Maddie's self-esteem was devastating. Her grades in other classes began to slip. Her social world began to shrink. She lost her enthusiasm for school, friends, and activities.

Parents are alarmed when their teenagers withdraw into a shell. Some parents recall their sons or daughters being enthusiastic and outgoing until a particular incident triggered a shutdown. Others with sons or daughters who have always been a little on the shy side worry that their shyness is keeping them from growing and experiencing life. Then there are those who are not so much withdrawn as they are caught up in maintaining an image. They spend a lot of time and energy being the tough guy, the glamour girl, or the most outrageous, and not much time being themselves. Some young people with low self-esteem are easily coerced by peer pressure into doing things against their will: drugs, bullying, and playing hooky. And there are those who pour a lot of energy into avoiding peer pressure. They conform to what they think is normal and avoid doing anything that might make them stick out.

The common thread among them is avoidance. Whether they withdraw, conform, or hide behind an image, they're trying to duck from somebody they don't want to deal with: themselves.

At the heart of this issue is negative self-image. For a kaleidoscope of reasons, teens can end up feeling bad about themselves—or about a particular aspect of themselves. They may become afraid to show their true selves—sometimes even to their parents.

Everybody goes through this kind of thing at some level. Most of the time it's an event or a phase. Other times, it's a downward spiral. That's when it becomes potentially damaging to teens—and terrifying to parents.

Not Perfect Equals No Good

Sometimes, when young people are exploring their identities and the way they present themselves to the world, they realize that they've gotten locked into the belief that they need to be perfect. They discover that they've been thinking in black and white. If they're not pretty enough, they're ugly. If they're too fat, too thin, or don't have the right clothes, they're worthless. They have to look good all the time or they'll be called out as losers.

When they explore what's motivating this obsession with being perfect, they often discover that it's fear. They're afraid their peers will judge them by their flaws—and often they're right.

What's perfection costing them? People who get onto the "perfect" track avoid situations that could expose them when they're looking less than perfect. They forget that when people are doing something for the first time, they're probably not going to do it perfectly—and they're going to look a little awkward while they're learning to do it. But since many are afraid of looking uncool, they shy away from trying anything new.

The bottom line is when teens obsess about perfection, they're focusing on things that have nothing to do with who they really are. When they realize that the unique, complex, terrific person inside them isn't getting a chance to be known, appreciated, or developed, they begin to look at their fear of social situations differently.

Conformity: Different Drummers Need Not Apply

"Why are you so weird?"

This is what a lot of young people hear when they're just being themselves. They may not realize that if they're being true to themselves, following their own interests, sometimes they're going to stick out. Sometimes they'll be zigging when everybody else is zagging. That's called being an individual. But in a teen's world, sticking out can attract a lot of negative attention.

Every culture has rules about conformity. A social scientist would probably explain that some kind of pressure is needed to hold people to an agreed-upon standard of behavior. But it can also hold them back. In Russia, young people who excel or show a lot of personality may be told, "Don't be a tall poppy." The first time we did our program in Russia, parents came to us afterward with tears in their eyes, so excited to see their children going for a higher level of achievement, no longer worried about whether anyone thought they were tall poppies.

Duncan, a Chinese student, wrote us that when he was younger he was always asking questions and inventing things, keeping a pretty high profile in a culture that discouraged standing out. So many of his classmates thought he was weird that over time he became timid.

Teens may not realize that when they give in to this pressure they're turning away from their own uniqueness. As a result, they don't follow the interests, hobbies, and passions that make them who they are. They don't develop their unique points of view, personal styles, or individual contributions. And there's another downside to conformity—they don't learn to see the value of diversity, in themselves or in others.

Duncan grew up according to the traditions and culture of his Chinese family. They were the same values taught at his conventional Chinese school in Hong Kong. Those values taught conformity: Don't stick out. Do what everyone else does.

Duncan wanted to break out of the mold. When he was fourteen he would crouch in his middle school stairway and scribble weird drawings of "my new inventions." Now and then he would look up to see if his classmates were giving him odd looks. They didn't like him because he wasn't playing by the rules. In a society that demanded answers, Duncan asked questions. It got to the point that teachers asked him to stop raising his hand because he would ask questions that had nothing to do with the day's topic.

Slowly, he became timid about expressing his thoughts and questions. He started to doubt his logic and decisions. He kept his views to himself and forced himself to conform. But the more he gave in, the less he liked himself.

Duncan's parents heard about an American camp that helped children with Duncan-type issues. This camp did amazing things with children's grades and self-esteem. His parents agreed to give it a try. Duncan was going to SuperCamp.

Like most campers, his transformation from insecure to confident happened gradually. At first he was awed by the dynamic curriculum and participants'

diverse cultural backgrounds. Traditional Chinese middle school taught him to follow the norm, but he couldn't find it at this camp. He became aware that people and education could be different. Through the camp's techniques and programs, he realized the importance of diversity in thought and culture. He became more confident in his decision-making abilities. He began to realize that he possessed the power to become his own person.

No more would Duncan let certain social conventions hold him back from having a great life. He transferred to an international school in Hong Kong to continue his exposure to diversity. He made academic goals, found a summer internship, and started to embark upon pathways few have traveled.

Now, six years later, he's majoring in environmental studies, Chinese, and dance at Tufts University in Boston, Massachusetts. One day he told his mother he planned to skip a year of college to pursue a different dream. He said he wanted to work in China in the environmental field to understand Chinese culture and find ways to use this culture to help people connect to the environment. Reluctantly, she agreed.

Today, Duncan is in China teaching rural Chinese how to live prosperous lives without damaging the environment. He feels comfortable following unusual beliefs—as long as he has a clear purpose for them.

Fortunately, Duncan was able to use the experiences he went through in our program to embrace his uniqueness. He has since gone on to do amazing things. He's studied physics, dance, ecology, and several languages—and is now helping others discover their unique contributions.

Talk to the Mask

As teens explore their use of "masks" they discover that they sometimes choose to hide behind them rather than risk exposing their true selves. When they're not feeling sure of themselves, or when they feel vulnerable, they may find it easier to lose themselves in a mask than to show their real thoughts, feelings, and identities. Better to be criticized for your mask than to be criticized for who you are.

Some even feel as though they have to wear masks around their parents. They put on the face of the Dutiful Daughter, the Tough-as-Nails Linebacker, or the Ivy League Up-and-Comer just to get Mom and Dad's acceptance.

When they work with the concept of masking, they discover that masks are a lot like labels. Everybody has more than one. They have little or nothing to do with who a person really is. And they cover up the unique, complex, incredible individual underneath. But there's a difference. Labels are identities other people stick on us; masks are identities we stick on ourselves.

For teenagers, the idea of wearing a mask has a lot of appeal. Trying to be themselves, especially when they're not even sure who that is, is frustrating, messy, and scary. Wearing a mask is easy, convenient, and safe. But there's a downside: What if they wear that mask so long that they forget who's under it?

One SuperCamp mom wrote us that her son realized just how much he'd been affected by his own masking: "...he proceeded to tell us that we didn't know him at all, that he'd been so hidden behind his mask that *he* wasn't sure who he was anymore."

Like those who cave in to conformity or obsess over perfection, people who get into the habit of hiding behind masks are robbing themselves of opportunities to develop as individuals. To make matters worse, if they're making choices for themselves based on their masks instead of on their true desires, they could be leading themselves further and further down a path that's all wrong for them.

Bookworming

Program grad Ashley wrote us about the time she was laughing with friends in her fifth grade class when somebody told her, "Your laugh is stupid." That one comment triggered a change in Ashley. She became self-conscious about her laugh. She retreated into her books and became, in her own words, a nerd and a brain. Her friendships withered and her world got smaller. She told herself she could pretend to go anywhere within the worlds of her books, but those pretend worlds didn't help her grow or discover herself. She began to feel alone, left behind, invisible.

Over time Ashley found that, even though books are great, they make lousy places to hide. "I just love to read" from a socially withdrawn teen means about the same as "I just love food" from an overeater. The behavior has little to do with love and everything to do with avoiding pain.

Parents of young people who bookworm often worry that their sons and daughters are becoming unreachable. What if they never come out from behind that book? Parents see that opportunities for social development are passing by and they worry that the longer their teens wait to get back into socializing the more difficult it will be for them to catch up.

Young people who withdraw do miss out on a lot of opportunities to develop socially and academically. Since they're not forging connections with their peers, they're losing out on social skills. As they sink deeper and deeper into solitude, they get further out of the habit of speaking up for themselves and expressing their wishes.

They're also missing out on building the kind of support network everyone needs. If they don't have friends, who's around to tell them they're okay as they are?

It's an Inside Job

Negative self-image is an inside job. All of these symptoms of poor self-image—bookworming, conformity, masking, and obsession with perfection—are *self-inflicted*. They're also self-reinforcing. They tend to get harder to reverse over time.

One of the magical things about the process our campers go through is that it's always set in a context of choice. As they come to a deeper understanding of the ways they may be hiding from themselves, they also become deeply aware that they're choosing these behaviors. But if they're the ones choosing to hide behind a mask, that means they can choose to remove that mask whenever they want. They have all the power in this scenario.

The issue of negative self-image looks very different when you view it as a choice instead of a problem. For one thing, it puts the idea in a clearly definable context and keeps it a manageable size. Whatever we focus on expands. Our office accountant, Dawn Nelson, who races cars, explains that in racecar driving most of the accidents occur when drivers round the curves. Many amateur drivers, as they approach the turn, focus all their attention on not hitting the curve—and guess what happens? They smash right into it. More experienced drivers, as they approach the turn, look *beyond* the curve. When teens or parents view self-image as a major problem, their subconscious mind draws more attention and energy to it, making it loom larger than life.

Young people are empowered when they stop thinking of their self-image as a problem and begin calling it what it is: a choice. Instead of treating it as a big scary obstacle, they can treat it as one more thing to explore, ponder, and turn into whatever they want it to be.

When they realize the power of choice they have in their own lives, they begin to see that the way things are going for them today isn't inevitable. Rather than agonize over their past choices, they can focus on the choices they have before them *now*.

The painful situations that have caused them to doubt themselves are normal; they're part of life—and there will probably be many more of them in every teen's future. But they can recognize that the way they react to these events is a choice. They can put on a mask or not. They can conform or stick out. They can withdraw or plunge in.

With that power of choice comes an automatic turnaround in self-esteem. Choice is powerful. Control over one's life is energizing. When teens truly understand that they're the ones in the driver's seat of their own lives, you can read it in their posture. They stand taller. They hold their heads higher. They speak with a powerful new timbre in their voices. This is the kind of transformation we live to see in young people.

What Are My Masks?

As teens become more familiar with their own masks, they discover how they and those around them use masking to get by in everyday life. We all slip in and out of a number of roles each day. We all wear masks according to what we're doing and with whom we're interacting. A teen naturally acts like a different person when she's with her grandmother than she does when she's hanging with her friends. She doesn't behave the same way toward her principal as she does toward her little sister. Masks can help or hinder the way a person relates to the world—depending on how they're used.

What's your mask? When do you wear it?

"Whenever there are more than three or four people in a room, I put on the quiet, reserved mask," one teen volunteers. "But when it's just me and Cheryl, I'm the cut-up."

Nick

The principal told Nick and his mother to come into his office and sit down. Then he looked up at Nick's mother and politely told her that her son wasn't smart enough to enter their private high school.

It wasn't the first time they'd had to sit through a talk like this one. In middle school, administrators told her not to expect too much from her son. They told her that it would be best for Nick to go to public school and do what he could. Nick would have enough trouble in school, they said. It would be a poor choice for him to suffer the humiliation of failing a private school's challenging entrance exam.

In essence, the private school principal told her the same thing. Nick failed the first time and his mother wanted him to take it again. The principal didn't see the point. Even if he passed, there was no guarantee he would graduate. He thought a trade school would be Nick's best chance for success.

Nick made it to junior year, but his parents began to worry. He'd managed to pass, but he was very close to failing each time. They heard of SuperCamp and thought Nick should go. They told him the camp would strengthen his learning skills.

Camp scared him at first. There were a lot of new kids from all over the place. He didn't want to talk to any of them because they might find out that he was dumb and barely made it to his junior year.

He sat at a cafeteria table eating his lunch when a team leader named Buddy approached him. Buddy asked if he could sit down. He asked Nick what he thought about the *Simpsons* television show. They talked. Nick laughed. Finally, Buddy offered Nick his Boston cream pie.

Nick felt accepted talking to Buddy. He left the lunch and walked back into a SuperCamp classroom. Something had changed. Everyone seemed to want to support him, not "knock him down."

Nick passed junior year and graduated from the private high school. He went on to work at SuperCamp because, as he put it, "I wanted to give back to the place that gave me so much." Four years later Nick graduated, not from a trade school, but from the University of Toledo.

Nick admits there was a time when he thought about using drugs to make himself feel better about his life and joining a gang so he could have a feeling of acceptance. He realizes now that he'd been close to falling into an ugly downward spiral that could have ended with him in jail.

Instead, thanks to his new lease on life, Nick has a goal. He wants to become a public speaker in middle and high schools; to reach out to children who have been told they're dumb and shouldn't have big dreams. "People need to hear a message of hope," he said. "There are so many things that could get you down. You need hope to make things better. Every day brings a new reality. Kids need to get that message reinforced."

Nick still talks to Buddy, the friend who made hope possible for him.

They think about what their masks do for them: "My 'responsible-young-leader' mask got me that summer camp job," or "Whenever I wear the 'I-can-take-it' mask, the guys don't pick on me as much because I don't make as fun a target."

What are the costs? What does your mask cover?

"I don't have as much fun hanging with my girlfriends when I'm wearing the quiet reserved mask."

"When I act like a tough guy, I don't let the guys see that their comments really hurt. Maybe if they had a choice, they'd rather know when they're hurting my feelings."

"My 'responsible-young-leader' mask makes me feel like a faker. I feel like I just put it on to impress my parents. I wish they could be impressed by *me* instead of by a mask I put on."

What matters most in this process is that teens are looking inside themselves for the answers. Nobody can get them from simply being told. Those magical "Aha!" moments come from within.

FIMAGE

If we were to summarize in a word why people, especially teens, wear masks, it would be FIMAGE.

What's FIMAGE? It's short for Fear of Image.

You don't have to look far into a group of young people to see examples of all the things they do to create an image. It's in their clothing, music, language, attitude, hair, make-up, hobbies—even in their choice of friends. Why do people have an image? To keep themselves looking good. Some people spend a lot of time creating and preserving their image. They avoid things that make them look uncool; things that aren't good for their image. They fear damage to their image. That's FIMAGE.

SuperCamp grad Sarah Samuel wrote, "If you have FIMAGE, it means you aren't comfortable doing certain things because of fear of what other people will think of you. You don't have self-confidence and you're always worrying."

As teens go deeper into their exploration of their own FIMAGE, they come to a major realization—by constantly fearing what will happen if they don't maintain their image, life will pass them by. If they want to branch out, try new things, and find out who they really are, *they have to let go of their image!*

Camper Dominique DeRoche told us, "It was hard at first to let

---

Ning

It's the ninth day of SuperCamp in Claremont, California. One hundred twenty teens sit impatient but silent, focused on the stage.

On the edge of the stage, a girl grips her brother's hand, terrified. She lets go of his hand and grabs her mentor's hand.

"Breathe," the mentor says.

Ning takes a deep breath. Her mentor whispers, "It's all you."

She lets go of her mentor's hand and walks to the center of the stage, fighting for even one more second to silence her fear.

She takes a deep breath and begins to speak.

"I am Ning. One thing I value in my life is who I am, and I will show this by being true to myself and showing my true self to others."

Trembling, she reaches up and removes the wig she's been wearing.

With her bald head revealed, she continues. "This is who I am."

For the last seven years Ning's been fighting alopecia, the rare skin disease that attacks hair follicles. In a world that values physical beauty, the disease is a devastating blow to a person's self-esteem.

Wig in hand, Ning returns to her seat, crying. Around her, stunned campers go silent. Then they erupt in a roar of support. They accept her for who she is—and admire her for the courage she's just shown.

Her mentor later says that the aspect of life he values the most is "that funky feeling you get in your stomach when you know someone has done something good or that you've done something good for someone."

By letting go of her FIMAGE, Ning has just taught a roomful of teens the true meaning of beauty.

go of FIMAGE, but it made me feel better after I let go, and now I'm not paranoid about how I appear to people."

In our process, teens have the opportunity to do some wacky things in front of their peers to practice letting go of their FIMAGE. In the context of a bunch of fun high-energy games, they can make crazy faces, ridiculous sounds, or fall on the carpet writhing and screaming. Nobody can look cool doing these things—that's the point. They can have the experience of looking uncool in front of their peers and being totally okay with it. We facilitators do it with them, so it's all a big group experience. We take it to the extreme so they know they can take it to the middle on their own. In the end they realize that not only did they not get ridiculed or rejected, they actually had a lot of fun.

Teens speak with a lot of enthusiasm about life beyond FIMAGE. "Letting go of FIMAGE makes your life greater because you let go of the insecurities you have about what others think of you," camper Bre Steinbarth told us. "You open up and let others see you without your mask. I created my own style, and I'm not afraid to act like myself and talk to other people."

"It feels good letting go and being able to be a 'weirdo' and have no one judge you," wrote camper Joe Dugan.

Camper James Ohnoki told us, "It's like taking a 100-pound bag of rice off your shoulders, like finally being free after being chained to a tree."

Camper Jordan Walton said, "I was able to show who I truly was for the first time."

Where the Thrill Isn't

Everybody's familiar with the concept of the comfort zone. It's where we live most of the time. Campers describe what it's like inside their comfort zones: comfortable, safe, familiar, and...*boring*.

"If life inside your comfort zone is boring, then where is life exciting?"

Outside the comfort zone!

As they explore their comfort zones, they realize that it's a great place to feel safe, but no learning or growing can take place there. *Outside* the comfort zone is the only place where they can take risks, discover, meet people, have fun—and learn.

Masking, bookworming, conformity, and FIMAGE are about staying inside the comfort zone. They're buffers between us and the exciting parts of life. When teens think of it this way, life outside the comfort zone appeals to their sense of adventure. They're not into boring. They like excitement.

Life Outside the Zone

Teens know what it's like outside their comfort zones. They've all been there. And they've all had positive experiences there: the first time they tried to rollerblade, drive a car, sing karaoke. They recall that these moments were uncomfortable, awkward, even a little scary. But what a rush it was when they discovered *they could do it!*

Campers who understand the difference between life inside and outside their comfort zones understand that they can't go for these incredible experiences and stay anonymous behind their images, beneath their masks, or with their noses in a book. It doesn't work. They understand that they have to let go of how they look if they want to take on the adventure.

Once they've spent time exploring this idea they're hungry to experience life outside their comfort zones firsthand. One of our traditions is to put on a familiar piece of music while campers form a circle. It's a team-building, energizing activity where teens have an opportunity to dance across the circle in whatever manner they choose. For some it's the first time they've been fully themselves in a long time.

This Is It!

Stepping outside the comfort zone is all about seizing the moment—

grabbing whatever adventure the present has to offer. The Key of Excellence we call "This Is It!" is about being aware of the present moment—and always making the most it.

This key helps teens journey outside their comfort zones because it's all about embracing whatever life brings, even if—*especially* if—it isn't what they expected. When they apply this key they discover that when they're in the now, life is more exciting. When they're fully in the moment they're vibrant, alive, supercharged. They enjoy what they're doing more, get more out of it, and are better at it. As one teen put it, when you're committed to being in the moment, you're "riding life 'til the wheels fall off."

A program grad, Grayson, wrote that he drew a lot of strength from this key: "I've gained the power not to be so shy. I've learned that it's really a good thing for a guy to be open and sensitive. The key for me is This Is It! My life is fulfilled if I live each day as if it were my last."

Masks Off: Who Am I?

Once we had a seventeen-year-old at camp who was all about being the tough guy. He told us he was a cage fighter. He showed everybody that he could bend his ankle backward as a result of an injury he sustained while fighting. But then he spent some time in an environment that treated him as somebody beyond his tough-guy image. As camp progressed he took off his mask.

One night he revealed that he was passionate about music. When he played his guitar he was in a world where he could express his emotions. Toward the end of camp he replaced his name tag with one that read "Emo," short for "Emotional." He explained, "That's who I am. I'm all about music and feeling and expression." That's the person who had been hidden away under the tough-guy mask.

As teens emerge from their FIMAGE and step out from behind their masks, they discover that the real surge of confidence comes from getting to know the person who lives behind that mask. As they begin to explore who they really are, they make an incredible discovery: They're pretty wonderful. They *like* themselves. They can count on themselves. And they can find other people to like them and count on them. That's where the courage to live life without masks comes from.

As they dig deep into their own identities, they journal and discuss the answers to thought-provoking questions like, "Who are my three best friends—and why?" "What recent accomplishments am I most proud of?" and "Some things about me that, if you knew them, would help you understand me better..." The answers to these questions help them get to know themselves. It's a journey of discovery that will take the rest of their lives to complete. It's about taking little victories and building on them, about finding out the quirks and dreams and passions that make them unique and celebrating them, about falling in love with who they are. Within this process a downward spiral into negativity can be turned into an upward spiral into the stratosphere.

Ashley, the girl who was told in fifth grade that she had a stupid laugh, once laughed out loud when she was in our program. She immediately checked herself, as had become her habit, afraid she would be ridiculed. Only this time nobody made fun of her. In fact, during a share later that day, one of the other campers said Ashley's laugh was one of the things they liked most about her. It made her unique. It's pretty hard for anyone to stay feeling bad about themselves when they're surrounded with so much evidence to the contrary.

All young people have the potential for greatness. Incredible things happen when they get a chance to see that greatness for themselves—and to have other people acknowledge them for it.

CHAPTER 4
Turning Fear of Disruptive Change into Accepting Change

When Charlie's parents divorced, his mom, Regina, noticed that he had a tough time coping with his dad's absence. His father, Charles, tried to stay involved in Charlie's life but his military career often required him to ship out for duty to bases around the world, and he was gone for months at a time.

Then one afternoon three military men came to the door. Charlie's dad had been killed in a helicopter crash. It wasn't the crash that had killed Charles but the fire afterward. The story left haunting images in Charlie's mind.

With the loss of his dad, Charlie seemed to go into hibernation. Regina watched helplessly as he withdrew from his friends, gave up on schoolwork, and sank into a depression.

Regina spent a lot of time talking to Charlie to find out exactly what was going on inside him. She was surprised to find out that he resented his dad for dying. Charlie wished he could tell his dad, "You were hardly there for me when you were alive, and now you won't be there for me at all."

As if being a teenager isn't challenging enough! Sometimes teens find themselves facing massive changes. Divorces, serious illnesses, a death in the family, moving to a new home, and other traumatic events can rock an already rocky world.

To a young person the death of a family member can seem impossible to deal with—particularly since relationships between many teens and their families are already on shaky ground. When a parent dies they may feel that all the unresolved stuff between them is now going to haunt them forever. Deeper still, they may be frightened about who's going to take care of them and how they'll get the parenting they need: "Where will I turn when I need a dad?"

A divorce can leave young people feeling abandoned and resentful. They may blame themselves for their parents' split-up. They might have trouble adapting to two different homes with two different sets of rules and may not know what's expected of them. They might feel as though time they're spending with one parent means they're being disloyal to the other parent. Even the most peaceful divorce can bring on big changes in the environment they count on for safety and acceptance—at a time in their lives when they feel a great need for stability.

A serious illness or injury can upset their lives, too. A young person might resent the changes in her daily routine that the illness is forcing on her—and then feel guilty for her resentment. If the family member needs special care, she might have a tough time handling the burden. A lot of scary thoughts might be going through her mind: "What if Mom doesn't pull through?"

Even a move to a new home can throw them into an emotional tailspin. Since their world is so full of new challenges and insecurities, they depend on home to be their safety zone. They rely on the security and familiarity of home and established routines to balance out the storminess of life as a teenager. When everything at home is strange and new, they can end up feeling as though there's no retreat for them. And on the social scene, it's hard enough to feel confident even when they have a few friends to back them up. When they're the new kid, it's like taking the usual social awkwardness and cranking the volume all the way up.

In our programs, a lot of the process teens go through is inner work: They explore their feelings, identify their thoughts, tap into events that have affected them, and find out what's making them behave the way they do. The bulk of what comes up is day-to-day stuff: "My best friend told me off. My mom wouldn't let me get my learner's permit." But from time to time, it gets heavy: death, divorce, serious illnesses—the kinds of things that can turn an adult's world upside down.

We're very clear about the fact that we don't do therapy. None of the things we do with teens is meant to take the place of a therapist's care. But when kids bring up personal tragedies, radical changes, or other events that have affected them in a big way, we listen. What we've heard from many campers suggests that they can sometimes attach their identities to a traumatic event—or they think it may be their fault. They might blame a family member for what happened and then let their resentment poison the relationship. They may not know how to overcome the tidal wave of emotion the event has unleashed, and may not even recognize what emotions they're experiencing. They could be ashamed to admit some feelings—even to themselves. These are some of the reasons they often respond to radical change by withdrawing, acting out, or shutting down.

The self-determination that teens discover in various parts of our process can help them cope with traumatic change. Even though massive changes can temporarily derail their lives, they're able to get themselves back on track when they realize they have a lot of power to affect their own lives. They know that nobody can control everything that happens to them, but something inside them transforms when they realize that they can totally control *how they think about* what happens.

The Home Team

Especially during tough times, young people need to know they can talk freely with someone they trust to really listen—someone who they feel is "on their team." Trust and security are created through acceptance, traditions, sharing, and a sense of belonging. They open up so freely and talk so deeply in our programs because we create this environment. Everything we do is on purpose.

We've learned that there's also an element of timing. Young people don't open up and share their feelings until they're ready. Nobody walks in on the first day of our programs and starts talking about emotions. When something traumatic and life changing has occurred, a teen may not be ready to talk just because somebody is ready to listen. They share when they decide the time is right. It's our job to do what we can to help them get ready for that time. For a while maybe the only thing we can offer is, "I'm here if you want to talk about it."

When the time is right, it helps to begin a conversation about a serious event with a few open-ended questions. Here's one that helps a lot: "What questions do you have about what happened?" Some parents have said that once their teens had a chance to ask questions, get a little bit of perspective, and come to a better understanding of the event, they were okay.

Here's a phrase that comes in handy: "Tell me more." This statement is powerful because it shows interest and asks for more information in an open-ended way. A simple "tell me more" can help get the conversation flowing. Let's say a teen is having trouble adjusting to his parents' divorce now that his mom lives five hundred miles away. His dad asks what that experience is like for him, and he responds with, "Stinks."

"Okay. Tell me more."

After a moment, when he's convinced Dad really does want to hear more, he might begin to fill in more details.

Talking it out is a terrific way to begin separating from the event and sorting through feelings. But it's not the only way to get there. Campers spend time writing their thoughts and feelings in journals during our program. Something about expressing themselves with the written word helps process things on a much deeper level. In the privacy of their journals they're free to let it rip. They can write any-thing, say it any way they want, and it's all completely private. It's a great way to let off emotional steam.

Particularly for visual learners, drawing a picture of feelings can also help. Drawing is liberating. It taps into creativity. It helps them get a new perspective. They're free to express themselves any way they want: with colors, shapes, objects, animals, people—anything goes.

They also find it helpful to write a short story about the event. Educator Michael Grinder says it sometimes helps people to talk about themselves in third person to avoid identifying themselves with the situation: "When Melodie was fourteen years old, she moved from the school she loved to a new school where she didn't know anybody…"

Some have found that it helps a lot to write a letter to the person involved in the incident—whether they send it or not. Just being able to address the person directly gets the feelings moving. That's a large part of why the parent talk helps. Even if—especially if—the person has passed on, the letter is a chance to express everything that remains to be said: "Dear Dad, there are a lot of things I wish I had told you before you went away…." Since the letter doesn't have to be sent, they don't have to hold anything back.

All Yours: The Power to Reframe It

Teens find there's power just in getting a handle on how they feel about a painful situation. Just understanding what's going on inside brings a little bit of peace. But the real transformation takes place when they take charge of the way they respond to what's happened.

As they work through their feelings about traumatic events in their lives, they discover that they've made choices along the way. Some ways of responding to an event diminished them. Some made them stronger. Which responses they chose were up to them. When they come to this realization they discover that in the future they can choose responses that have a better outcome. When it comes to their responses to an event, the power is all theirs.

Once we had a teen who made a bad choice while he was in the program. He blamed his behavior on the fact that his parents were divorcing. We explained to him that no matter what was going on with his parents, his behavior was still his own choice. He came to see that he could control his emotions. He could move himself up to a better place—and even take other people up with him sometimes.

The principle behind this idea is Ownership, one of the most powerful of the 8 Keys of Excellence. Taking Ownership means taking responsibility for your actions. Campers really understand this key when they think of it in terms of "pride of ownership," the way they felt about the first special thing they owned. When they realize they can feel that same pride of ownership about their behavior, their whole attitude changes. Owning their actions puts them in control. It allows them to move their lives in the direction they choose instead of being a passive recipient of someone else's choices. When they take ownership, they're in control.

Ownership becomes an even more powerful tool during tough times. Taking ownership of the way a traumatic event affects them means they have a choice in a situation that seems otherwise out of their control.

What choices do they have? During our programs teens play the Ownership Game to learn more about the kinds of choices they make every day. In any given situation, everybody chooses behavior that's either Above the Line or Below the Line. Whenever they're making excuses, laying blame, justifying, or giving up, they're playing Below the Line. When they take responsibility, look for solutions, or follow through on plans, they're playing Above the Line. They learn that playing Below the Line brings penalties like powerlessness, lack of trust, and loss of freedom. Playing Above the Line brings rewards like freedom, trust, respect, and success.

Campers who play the Ownership Game make a breakthrough discovery. Even in the most traumatic circumstances, when their lives seem to be in chaos, they still have control over one thing: *They can still decide how they're going to respond!*

Still Got that Rock in Your Shoe?

Playing Above the Line means choosing positive attitudes and behaviors—and letting go of destructive ones. Young people sometimes respond to emotional pain by hanging on to resentment—blaming another person for their pain. They may resent one or both parents for a divorce or for moving them away from their old home. They might even blame a parent for dying and leaving them. But the tricky thing about resentment is that it hurts us even more than it hurts the person we resent.

One teen told us that she held a lot of resentment toward her father who wasn't around much after her parents divorced. Her new stepfather was involved in her life and came to all of her events but she kept him at arm's length for fear that if she got close to him he would abandon her too. She realized that by not allowing herself to get close to her step dad she was hurting herself, and missing out on the close relationship that *was* available.

When they're able to see it this way, they understand that resentment is a Below the Line choice. But it's not always easy for them to let go of resentment if they've been carrying it around a while.

"How many of you have ever been hiking and gotten a rock in your shoe?"

Most respond with a nod. *Been there. Done that. Ow.*

"Resentment is just like that rock. Rather than take your shoe off and remove the rock, you wiggle the stone around in your shoe until you find a place where it doesn't hurt as much. Then you leave it there. Instead of telling people about our feelings, we wriggle them off to the side, hoping they'll get better."

The campers are still nodding. Some are laughing. Most of them can see themselves in this story.

"...But pretty soon the yucky feeling slips back up just like the rock. Eventually, your foot goes numb. Once you're in a dull, numb state, resentment starts wearing a hole in your soul too."

All around the room, you can practically see light bulbs going on in their heads. They totally get it. They realize that just like they do with the rocks they keep in their shoes on a hike, they're putting that pain on themselves. Resentment is pain they volunteer for. They can make it stop any time they want!

We love moments like that. When you're as obsessed with teen success as we are, times like these make it all worthwhile.

There's another powerful process campers go through when they're exploring resentment. If you're willing, try this experiment with us.

"Okay, squeeze both your fists together," the facilitator says. "Squeeze hard. Really hard. Like you're gripping a rock."

All around the room we see clenched fists and scrunched faces. They're really squeezing.

While they keep squeezing, the facilitator says, "That squeezing sensation is like the resentment you're carrying. Now think about the person you resent. *What if they never change?*"

When we look around the room we see a lot of grimaces. By now the campers *really* want to stop squeezing their fists. But it's not time to let go yet.

"Look at your hands—what color are they?"

"Red," they say through clenched teeth.

"And what color would you give the emotion of anger and hurt?

"Red!"

The tighter they squeeze the more pain they feel. By now most of the teens are *really* aware that they're doing this to themselves. Just as they're the ones making themselves feel bad when they hold on to resentment.

A few minutes later we ask them to look at their hands again—what color are they now?

"Purple," they grunt, "white."

"And why is that?"

"Because the blood has left my fists."

"And how does that feel?"

"Numb."

"Exactly. Numb. Dead. Just like our relationship with that person goes dead if we hang onto resentment long enough."

Finally we let them release their fists. What do they feel now?

"Relief!"

"Just like the relief we feel when we forgive someone."

Campers connect deeply with these resentment processes because they build on information they already have. Emotions are tricky for them to deal with because they're intangible—they're hard to measure and define. But they've all had rocks in their shoes. They all feel the pain of squeezing their fists. First they have the experience. Then they label it. By the time they find out what they're learning, they've already learned it. Pain is there until you release it. Resentment is there until you decide to let it go.

But where does resentment come from in the first place? When they explore this question, they realize that it comes from other people not meeting their expectations. Not doing what they think they should do. When we resent someone for not meeting our expectations, we call it "shoulding" on them.

Campers spend some time talking about the reasons people might not act the way they expect them to. Maybe they just don't know any better. Maybe their behavior makes sense to them.

They recognize the difference between letting go of shoulding and condoning bad behaviors. Obviously there are some behaviors that are definitely not okay. But letting go of resentment isn't about *accepting* behavior; it's about not accumulating bad feelings over what somebody else chooses to do.

Facing the FEAR

Another Key of Excellence that helps teens through rough times is Flexibility. Being flexible is all about learning to handle change. It's about getting off what's not working and looking around for what does work. Life has a habit of throwing curve balls from time to time. When situations don't go the way you'd planned, you can stay rigid and stick with behavior that doesn't work anymore—or you can let go and do something different.

Once when we were talking about flexibility, one of the facilitators told the campers about the time she was getting married and expected the perfect wedding—which turned out to be anything but. The room was too hot and her husband-to-be fainted. She explained that even though it wasn't all that amusing when it happened, the situation was saved when they stopped obsessing about how their plans were ruined and instead managed to find some humor in it. It ended up making a good story that they'll be telling their family for years to come.

Campers become aware that flexibility is not about randomly changing things for the heck of it, but about recognizing the behavior or attitude that's keeping things from working the way they want. It's hard to admit when something we're doing isn't working. We get our egos wrapped up in what we're doing. But if we don't like the results we're getting, the only thing we can change is *our own behavior.*

Everybody's scared of change—even adults. Doing things the same old way *feels* easier—even when it isn't. It takes courage to face change, whether we choose it voluntarily or have it thrust upon us by circumstances. We fear the unknown—and we often expect the worst. In our program, FEAR stands for False Expectations Appearing Real. Campers are often scared of what could happen if they speak in front of a group, make themselves visible, or put themselves in a position where others might see them fail. But really, what *is* going to happen? They have a real epiphany when they discover that, most of the time, nothing happens that's worthy of the kind of fear they give it.

What really gives teens a surge of confidence is realizing that when they do something worthwhile in spite of their fears, the fear goes away!

Many also find that some disruptive change leads to something better. They realize that if it weren't for the change, they wouldn't be as strong, or wouldn't have found a new relationship, wonderful neighborhood, or great school. Sometimes change brings opportunities, even though it feels scary or unfair at the time. When they recognize that change may bring all kinds of experiences, not just negative, frightening ones, they're able to face it from a different point of view.

Healing, Growing, and Moving On

Even though terrible things sometimes happen, young people can move forward with confidence knowing that they can decide how to respond to whatever life throws at them. It's about taking a painful event and getting to a place of healing—of being able to learn from it, get stronger, and keep on rising to the challenge of living.

CHAPTER 5

Turning Poor Grades into Excelling in School

Last year at the end of the school year we did a little dance because Cody made it to the next grade. For quite a while there, we weren't sure if he would. He's a bright kid, but schoolwork just seems to frustrate him. I'd come to think of him as a poor learner. My highest expectations were that he might one day work his way up to being a C student...

Why is schoolwork such a struggle for so many teens? We believe the main reason is that most are never taught how to learn. When they *are* taught learning skills, they respond with, "Why didn't anyone tell me this? It makes so much sense to me now!" Until they have the basic common-sense tools of learning, they won't have the opportunity to discover how great they are.

Aside from lack of learning skills, many young people get turned off to schoolwork for a bunch of reasons that have nothing to do with their true academic ability. Maybe a string of failures has led them to develop self-defeating attitudes. They might have different learning styles than the ones their teachers are using. Their teachers may not be showing them why the subjects they're teaching matter—they may not relate to the material. They may have come to think of school as another thing adults are imposing on them—or something that gets handed to them rather than something they go after. Or maybe they're just bored.

Something often seems to happen in the teen years to extinguish the joy of learning that came naturally to them—as it does to all of us—when they were small. Without that love of learning there's little motivation for them to do well in school.

How can young people recapture their love of learning? How do they get motivated from within? How do they find out just how much they're capable of? How can they transform that apathy into enthusiasm?

It's a thrill when teens wake up to the possibility of owning their learning processes. As they discover how they learn, it hits them why certain approaches don't work well for them—and why other approaches work great. They also learn some basic skills of learning, memorizing, and studying, and working their way through a series of small victories that boost their confidence. Skills, combined with a take-charge attitude, catapult teens' academic performance in a whole new direction.

What's School Like for My Teen?

We learn a lot from parents. They often observe how much easier it is to talk about school with their sons and daughters after SuperCamp. Before, when parents brought up the subject of school-work, their teens tended to get reactionary: "Here it comes: the big lecture. It's all for my future, yadda yadda." But after camp, many of them can hardly *stop* talking about their school experiences.

Most of the time, young people live in the moment. Many can't connect with the idea that what's unpleasant for them today will help them tomorrow. When adults tell them their school performance is important to their future, it's probably not going to mean a lot to them. Unless they see what it's going to do for them *today*, they probably won't pour themselves into it. A few teens have the opposite problem. They're so intensely focused on getting the grades, prepping for their university careers, and being perfect students that they're missing the joy of the experience. They're viewing their education too narrowly.

Our interactions with teens work because we come from their point of view. The "I-did-it-why-can't-you" type of story that adults often fall back on—with the best of intentions—doesn't help teens much when they're struggling. These anecdotes can make them feel as though they don't measure up. For many, they might make the situation worse. Fear of failure can sabotage academic performance.

And what about the teen who's getting As and Bs? What help does she need with school? That depends. What's she really getting out of her education? Is she learning to learn, or is she mostly learning to get grades?

High grades aren't the goal of education; they're byproducts. Excellent grades *are* important—especially when it comes to getting into a great school. But a bright young person can get so focused on grades and test scores that she misses the bigger picture. Here's a better question: How well can she apply what she's learning? Can she take a paradigm from one subject and use it to help her learn another? How creatively can she manipulate the knowledge she has? Is she doing extracurricular activities to round out her education? And, especially, is she having fun?

We focus on finding out how each teen sees school. What's it doing for them? How do they see themselves in the process? Sometimes all they want is to be heard and understood—and left to work things out in their own way. Other times, talking through their experience can help them discover where something's missing—holes in their school skills that need to be filled or places where their attitudes could use a little adjusting. Instead of us telling them what we think they need, they explore it for themselves.

The impact is much greater when *they're* the ones to identify what needs to change.

Tests? Bring 'em On!

What comes up for you when you hear the word "test"? *I'll never make it. I'm going to fail. I need to go to the nurse.* These are typical responses we hear from students.

Over the years, young people develop certain attitudes about school. Their attitudes are made up not just of the actual experiences but also of everything they've thought about these experiences. Events they might have perceived as being unpleasant, like tests, get reinforced as negatives because they fall into the habit of thinking of them in negative terms.

The human brain listens to what it's being told and forms itself accordingly. Every time we relive an unpleasant experience or think a negative thought, we're strengthening the neural connections that lead to the "tests–are–awful" conclusion. But what if a teen decides to replace that connection with a different one? One that says, "Tests are cool. I'm totally into them. I love the challenge."

When teens are exploring their attitudes about school, we tell them whenever somebody says the word "test" they can yell, "C'mon! Gimme that test!" It's fun—and it also changes the way they think about tests. By transforming their attitudes from "oh no, not a test" to "bring it on!" they're rewiring their brains to welcome academic challenges instead of fearing them. Instead of being the passive victims of tests, they *own* the whole testing experience!

One time a school superintendent was visiting one of our programs. She was talking to one of the facilitators and casually mentioned the word "test" in conversation. She jumped when a dozen campers standing nearby shouted in unison, "Gimme that test!"

The Ownership key is where we come from when we talk academics. It's easy for young people to slip into a passive role: "The teacher teaches; I just sit here and absorb." By the time they hit their teen years, a lot of kids have switched to autopilot in school. The stuff they're learning is inert because they're barely interacting with it.

But something exciting happens when people reclaim ownership of their education. They rediscover the fun and challenge of learning. They become the captains of their own experience instead of being benchwarmers. Now they can direct where their education goes—and how far.

Taking ownership of their education means no more excuses, never playing the blame game again: "She made me do it." "He's not a good teacher." "My study partner's not good at math." "This school's lame." Ownership is about taking 100% responsibility for everything that we do and where we are in life. Period.

When young people take back the responsibility for their academic performance, their energy levels automatically go up. You can see pride of ownership in a person's eyes and read it in their posture. Just taking ownership gets them more engaged, more enthusiastic, more awake and more alert.

Program grad David Evans told us how the Ownership key helped him revive a sagging GPA: "I totally got how I could take command and harness my capabilities. The following school year I was sitting next to my friend in honors chemistry. We used to sit in class and we would spend most of the time cracking jokes and making fun of the teacher. I suddenly realized that my old behaviors wouldn't fit into my new beliefs. I wanted to pay attention in class. I told my friend, and it really caught him off guard, but that didn't stop me. From that moment on, there was no looking back for me."

One of the signs campers read on our walls says, "I Am Responsible for What I Create." Once they realize they're in charge, they're on their way to greatness. When they couple ownership with a can-do attitude and some nuts-and-bolts learning skills, they're an unstoppable express train to success!

Can Do! Why the Success Model Works

Campers come out of our programs sparkling with confidence because they've come face to face with their own success. We don't leave it to chance, belief, or wishful thinking. We let them experience for themselves just how good they are. We build in opportunities for them to succeed. They don't just believe they can be successful, they *know* it—because they've done it.

Teens shouldn't have to miss out on achievements because they're afraid they'll fail. They're afraid to find out they can't do something. They tell themselves, "As soon as I feel good enough about myself, I'll try something big." But what we've found by working with teens is that self-confidence works exactly the opposite way. It comes from going after something aggressively—and achieving it. It's a matter of starting small, of going for little successes and building from there.

Campers break through the self-confidence barrier over and over again with the help of what we call the Success Model. We use this strategy throughout our programs, not just for academics but for life skills, attitude—you name it. Campers first experience small private successes, then work their way up to giant public ones. All along the way, they're building on what they know they can do—with the help of lots of repetition and practice. We *rehearse* for success. They use the energy of their previous success to catapult them into the next.

"Before I attended SuperCamp, I wasn't challenging myself in school. I was in only one advanced placement course. I was a member of student council and the golf team, but I was not in any leadership roles. This all changed after SuperCamp. I attacked my junior year with my SuperCamp skills and the results have been very positive. I have excelled in school and extracurricular activities. For my junior year I earned a grade point average of 98 out of a possible 100. SuperCamp taught me that this is my life, right now! I was just letting my high school career slip by without doing anything. It's amazing how much one person can do, and how happy one person can make other people. Since SuperCamp, I've become much more optimistic and confident about myself. I've learned to pick out the positive things and forget the negative things, to focus on my good qualities rather than worry about my bad ones."

—Austin Woody

For instance, when we work through memorization skills, the first things we do are large-group callouts where they can stay anonymous if they're afraid they don't know the answer. It's very safe. Next we practice in small groups or pairs, leading up to individual performance which can be a teen speaking or performing alone in front of the group, or in some cases the individual performance of taking a test.

Where they fear to go in one giant step, they can go with confidence in a series of small steps, each built on the foundation of a previous success.

ABCs: Not Just for Preschoolers Anymore

We love it when we get letters from SuperCamp graduates about their academic breakthroughs. They understand and remember a lot more, their grades have improved, and their SAT and college entrance scores have gone up. These are some of the end results of a process that begins with the way they think about themselves. We hold these truths to be self-evident: Every person is a capable learner, people learn in different ways, and learning happens best in a fun, engaging, and challenging environment.

To get these principles firmly in mind, teens learn their ABCs:

A is for Attitude: What we tell our minds about something in advance will affect the outcome. When young people approach their education from a "This Is It!" mindset and have an insatiable curiosity and a thirst for knowledge, they can learn just about anything. A "bring it on!" attitude makes learning easier.

B is for Belief: What we believe about our abilities affects our performance. If a person believes she's a poor learner, guess what? Her belief will be a self-fulfilling prophecy. But if she decides to tell herself, "I'm a good learner and I'm getting better every day," her ability to learn goes up. We all have the power to choose our beliefs—those who choose empowering can-do beliefs are much more likely to reach their goals.

C is for Commitment: There's awesome power in making a commitment. Once people lock on to a particular goal or course of action, they discover resources they didn't know they had. When they make a commitment to learning, their energies shift. It's like a giant lens that suddenly comes into focus.

I Hear You, I'm Catching On, I've Got the Picture

"My teacher hates me. She gets mad whenever I ask her to repeat something."

"When I told my teacher I had to read the same page over again three times to get what it said, he told me I was just being lazy."

"I got in trouble for fidgeting in my chair, but I just can't get what the teacher's saying if I sit still."

Young people often sense that there's a disconnect between them and their teachers, but they seldom know what's behind it. Frustrated teachers often assume that a student is being lazy or impertinent even though he or she is really trying to learn.

Often, what's going on here is that the student's style of learning is different from the teacher's style of teaching.

No two people learn exactly the same way. Some people learn better in one environment than another. Often, teens become convinced they *can't* learn when in fact they'd learn just fine if the information were presented differently.

Many school systems and teachers still aren't fully aware that different students learn in different ways. A one-size-fits-all teaching method is never going to reach every student. Sometimes teens get labeled with Attention Deficit Disorder when what's really going on is that the teacher doesn't know how to reach the student. We're not advocating against correct diagnoses and prescription drugs when they're appropriate—there are teens with

ADD whose meds have made their worlds good again—but it's possible that not all diagnoses of ADD are equally correct. When people get a handle on the way they learn, they can customize their learning experiences and fill in the gaps their teacher might leave.

Human beings have three main ways to take in new information: visual, auditory, and kinesthetic. For most of us, one of these ways is dominant and the other two are weaker.

Visual learners like to see pictures, colors, charts, and graphs. They usually do well with reading. They talk in visual terms like "picture," "view," "see," "look," and "vision." Visual learners like to sit in the front row, looking at the teacher and the board. They take good notes but sometimes miss the oral parts of the lecture.

Auditory learners like words that have to do with sound such as "hear," "listen," "tune," "ring," "chime," and "music." Auditory people are the ones mentally recording everything the teacher is saying but often looking away. They're often repeating what the teacher just said in the form of a question. Sometimes the frustrated teacher, not understanding what the auditory learner is doing, says, "That's what I just said. Weren't you listening?"

Kinesthetic learners learn by touch and movement. Words that appeal to kinesthetics are "feel," "sense," "handle," "do," "gut," and "intuition." Kinesthetic people like to feel things out, be emotionally connected, and learn by doing. Other people get annoyed at them because they can't seem to sit still, but they process information best by moving their bodies.

How do people know which kind of learners they are? There are tests they can take, but most get a pretty good sense of their learning styles just by becoming aware of the way they behave in class. They can also pay attention to the way they express themselves. If they "get it," "grasp the problem," or "have a feel for" a certain subject, they're probably strongly kinesthetic. If a phrase "rings true" or "sounds familiar," they're likely to be high-auditory.

If they "see what you mean," or "get the picture," they're probably visual learners.

Visual learners can help themselves stay connected to the lessons by sitting where the teacher will be in their immediate visual field. They learn best by reading or seeing a thing being done before they try it themselves. They absorb more information when they use lots of colors and graphics in their notes.

Auditory learners can boost their learning by reading lecture notes out loud. They learn best by having something explained to them verbally before they try it. It helps them to talk to a parent or friend.

Kinesthetic learners want to try something for themselves before they have it explained to them. Since touch is important, kinesthetics learn better when they incorporate movement and physical objects into their lessons.

Jolie struggled all the way through high school, believing something was wrong with her. Whenever she had to write a paper, she couldn't seem to put her thoughts into written words. She'd gotten used to teachers giving up on her. Then one teacher, who had assigned a paper comparing the students' generation to their parents', pulled Jolie aside and said, "You can approach this assignment any way you want. You don't have to write the entire thing. You can do some of it as a comic strip, a series of photos, a collection of memorabilia—whatever really gets you into the subject." For the first time, Jolie was able to approach an assignment from a hands-on perspective. Though she still struggled with the written part, she found that snapping photos of her friends interacting with their parents and drawing cartoons to illustrate different scenarios between adults and teens brought the material to life. Jolie's paper turned out so well that the teacher recommended that it be published in a special edition of the school's newsletter.

Campers who have come to believe they're poor learners have a major "Aha!" when they realize they learn just fine *in their own way.* In many cases, it's not that they can't learn, it's that the way they learn and the way the teacher teaches aren't a match! Once they have this information, teens can take charge of their learning again and fill in what's missing from their learning environment.

Notes: Why Just Take 'em When You Can Make 'em?

Sometimes young people fall behind in class because they have trouble taking useful notes. Some think they have to copy down everything the teacher says verbatim. They write like crazy during lectures but still end up falling behind. Others miss the big picture of what's being said and focus on the wrong details. Still others take terrific detailed notes that are right-on but fail to think about how the information applies *to them*. They might ace the next test but the only thing they'll take away from the experience is a bunch of lifeless facts.

Note-taking is a lot like studying; everybody's expected to do it, but nobody's ever taught how. Young people often develop a negative attitude about note-taking because it's boring. But it doesn't have to be. Somewhere along the line, they got in the habit of thinking that the purpose of note-taking was just to record the information that was being handed to them. But notes can also be a place to work out *what they think about* the content being taught.

Campers can develop their skill of a note-taking method we call Notes: TM, which stands for Taking and Making. With Notes: TM, they make a column two-thirds of the way across the page. The left-hand column is for Taking notes, the right is for Making them. On the left, they can record the information. On the right, they record how they think, feel, and relate to what they've just been taught. We encourage them to use colors, symbols, whatever they can think of to make it fun and personal.

This kind of note-taking works because it's interactive. People generally learn things best when they see themselves or make an emotional connection to the material. Their education counts the most when they find ways to be active learners instead of passive recipients.

Taking Breaks Helps Me Learn?

We like breaks. We take lots of them because we understand the role they play in the learning process. Did you know taking breaks at the right intervals can actually help you learn better?

We learn best at the beginning and end of a learning session. So the more we break our learning into chunks, the more optimal learning moments we create for ourselves!

People stay fresh longer if they build short breaks into their study routines. Even a quick pop-up from the computer to do a couple of laps around the room or a few jumping jacks can allow them to return to their studies refreshed.

Map It, Color It, Hang It Up for Review

The purpose of studying is to help our brains *process* the information we've learned. It's not just about cramming facts into our memory banks; it's about getting it in there in a usable, meaningful, retrievable form. Instead of memorizing a bunch of dry facts, students can study by manipulating the information in all kinds of fun ways.

There are tons of ways active learners can help their brains process information. One of our campers' favorites is Mind Mapping®, a method developed by Tony Buzan in the 1960s. Mind Mapping is all about drawing and coloring and getting creative. It helps us learn things much more thoroughly because it involves both sides of the brain at once and lets us get the big picture of what we're learning. How do you Mind Map? You start by turning the page lengthwise (landscape) and putting one word or symbol that stands for the subject in the middle. Then you draw branches coming off that main idea, one for each important idea. Use symbols and colors wherever possible. Mind Mapping is a great way to organize a book report, study for a test, or plan an event. People have used it for all kinds of things from planning parties to solving problems.

Young people do better when they learn how to *work with* what they're getting in class. Those who manipulate their lessons—who play with the information, turn it upside-down, and put it in different contexts—make more use out of what they're learning. It's a lot tougher to call something boring when you've found half a dozen ways to put it to use.

For program grad James Ohnoki, Mind Mapping was a turning point in his school career. The visual elements helped him get the big picture, and the drawing and coloring gave him a chance to get his natural creativity in on the act. Suddenly, schoolwork became a much more interactive experience for him. His grades improved and his interests expanded. He found that he had more confidence to tackle anything he set out to do and learn.

A learning technique that really works with an individual's style can bridge the gap between student and coursework.

Outside the Box: Where Creativity Rules

New ideas don't come to closed minds. When we're working on creative problem solving we encourage campers to break themselves wide open, to suspend judgment, branch out, explore possibilities, and borrow from the world around them.

The best way to get new ideas is to gather up *a lot* of ideas. Campers jump into this activity with big sheets of newsprint, piles of colored markers, and tons of energy. Sometimes they toss foot bags to one another or practice with juggling scarves to get the ideas flowing. At this stage there's no such thing as a bad idea. When they're idea gathering, they focus just on getting as many ideas as possible—no judging. Anything goes, even the silliest, most impractical ideas. Just throw it out there and see what happens. We call this divergent thinking. They just call it fun.

Once they've got a great collection of ideas, they can start narrowing down what they have until they're left with a handful of the very best ones. We call that convergent thinking. It's between these two processes, the expanding and squeezing, that new approaches to problems are born. We call the whole process "slinky thinking." From there it's about picking the best idea and turning it into action.

We've found that it really helps teens to have a few basic creative thinking techniques under their belts. That confidence makes a huge difference.

Whoa—My Brain Can Do *That?*

Many young people worry that their memories aren't up to the task when it comes to schoolwork. Here again it's a matter of training. Even though there are gazillions of ways to improve memory, schools don't do much to help students learn how to train their memories.

Fear of inadequate memory can become a self-fulfilling prophecy. The more people worry about their ability to remember, the less they focus on the information they're trying to remember. We help teens discover just how much they're capable of doing and provide them with strategies for getting information to stick in their brains. We use rhymes, songs, stories, colors, smells, people, even animals, associating items to remember with locations around the room, or characters in a movie. The goal is to find ways to give the material the strongest impact.

One of the best ways we've found to memorize a chunk of information is to tell it as a crazy story. Sometimes we tell campers the following story without explaining anything beforehand about what it means:

> You walk into a *deli* and order a sandwich and it comes to you with *pens* stuck in it. You say "Ugh!" and throw it out the window. It lands on a man's bright orange *jersey.* You go outside and apologize and the man yells, "By *George,* you've ruined my jersey!" You run away quickly and he can't come after you because his feet are *connected to cuts* in the sidewalk. To be sure you've escaped you duck into a nearby

Catholic church during a *Mass*. You duck out and go into a music store owned by *Marilyn*. You walk in and hear a *Southern carol* playing loudly on the stereo. Suddenly, out of the floor come hundreds of baby *new hamsters*. They pick you up and carry you off to a forest full of girls named *Virginia* playing harps. It's peaceful in the Virginia forest until the *New York* Yankees come out from behind the trees swinging. A ball is hit. You are hit by the ball. You're taken to a hospital where you have to wait in the *North Care line*. When you feel better, you jump out into traffic and barely make it to the *road island*. On that island you look down and see a bunch of disgusting *vermin* oozing up from the ground, sticking to your bare feet. You scream, "Oh, rats!"

Campers can easily memorize this story because of its absurdity and vivid details. Only after it's already in their heads do we reveal that they've also just learned the first fourteen states that ratified the U.S. Constitution—and the order in which they ratified it!

These memorization techniques work because they cause the information we're learning to have a greater impact on our brains. By attaching information to a rhyme, a body movement, a color, a bizarre image, a location, a sensory experience, or an emotion, we're anchoring the memory in our minds by more than one connection. We're getting more than one part of the brain in on the action by using visual, auditory, and kinesthetic strategies. Not only does it work, it makes memorization a lot more fun.

When teens realize how much their minds are really capable of, their confidence skyrockets.

Cracking the Learning Code

"Imagine you're standing in front of a safe with a combination lock. Inside the safe is a magical way to make studying faster and easier. But if you want to open this safe and claim the prize inside, you have to know the code. Put out your hand and grasp the dial on the front of the safe."

Putting a physical gesture to a piece of information makes mental retention *much* stronger.

"Now, spin that dial to the right until you come to number ten."

The campers crank their outstretched hands to the right.

"Okay, now spin the dial to the left until you see the number twenty-four."

They do it.

"And finally, spin it to the left until you come to the number seven."

They spin.

"Now hear the clicking sound of an opening lock. Imagine the door to the safe swings open and there's your prize: the ability to study better in less time. You can get into this safe any time you want. But you have to remember the code. What's the code?"

The teens shout back, "Ten, twenty-four, seven!"

That's it. The ten stands for ten minutes. The twenty-four is for twenty-four hours. The seven is for seven days. We've learned that these are the best intervals for reviewing new information. When we get new information, the best way to get it uploaded to our long-term memories is to review it ten minutes after we've learned it, then again in twenty-four hours, then once more a week later.

What's in it for them? Why is this code such a find? Because it cuts down on study time. It gets content uploaded into long-term memory—which means they're really learning the material, not just storing it in short-term memory then dumping it after the test is done. It's a magical recipe for making more time to have fun and hang with friends while still acing that test!

This Can't Be Schoolwork—It's Too Much Fun!

There's something that every teenager knew ten or twelve years ago when they were small children, but might have forgotten along the way. Learning is fun! We make sure fun is in the mix for everything we do, but especially in learning.

When young people step outside their comfort zones—into what we call the Learning Zone—it may be scary, frustrating, uncomfortable, embarrassing, and challenging. But it's never boring.

"Boredom," the facilitators say, "is a sign that learning is not taking place."

When students nurture a "bring it on!" attitude about their schoolwork, just the fact that the work is difficult and challenging is enough to make it fun. The fun comes from the thrill of overcoming something challenging and achieving something worthwhile. This is the attitude of a lifetime learner.

If you're bored you're not learning. If you're learning you're having fun. Fun is the necessary first ingredient in learning. It's where you get the motivation to charge into education with boldness and enthusiasm, which in turn opens the door to confidence and the development of learning skills.

One program grad told us, "I learned that when you're confident and know what tools to use, you'll win the game of school and life."

CHAPTER 6

Turning Lack of Focus
into Organized Study Strategies

*I have a really bright ADD son and I was frustrated that
this wonderful boy couldn't get any traction. We tried
everything: testing, therapy, counseling, you name it. David
was at a point in his life where he needed some tools to
manage the more chaotic parts of himself and to separate
the "noise" from what was important. He believed he had
to be the class clown in order to feel confident.*

"He's a smart kid; he just doesn't pay attention."

"She only wants to learn the subjects that interest her."

"It's in one ear and out the other with him."

"Her head's always in the clouds."

"He says schoolwork is boring. It's not supposed to be entertaining—it's school!"

"Her mind is like a sieve. She reads a book and can't remember a single thing."

We hear the frustration of parents whose children have "tuned out". They know their teenagers could do much better, but they can't seem to stay focused on anything. To parents, the lack of focus is particularly infuriating because it can look as if they're being rebellious. It's especially scary when it starts to look as though they *can't* concentrate—as though a learning disability or mental disorder might be the culprit.

Why do so many young people have such a hard time staying focused?

We understand that there are real disorders and syndromes like ADD that need to be treated medically. But most young people who have trouble concentrating don't have a medical problem; they're simply missing a few skills. Most don't concentrate well because they don't know how! Even kids with medically diagnosed concentration problems can benefit from gaining a few key skills. Concentration and focus have to be learned. Many haven't yet learned the basic skills of preparation, planning, and decision-making. They often tune out because they don't know how to approach an unfamiliar task or new chunk of information. What else can they do?

Teenagers see things differently than adults do. It's not just a lack of experience on their part; their brains really are different from adults'. They haven't yet fully developed their capacity for abstract thought.

Young people need experienced adults to provide them with the tools to develop their skills, to believe in their ability to master these skills, and especially, to understand what they're going through. When their kids are in trouble, parents want to make things all better. The problem is, in their haste to end their children's pain, parents "solve" their problems so quickly they often don't even take time to listen.

Young people are really trying to tell us something when they say, "I'm bored." It's not often a parent's first reaction to ask, "Why is my son bored? What's it like for him?" But by finding out more about their experience, we can best know how to help them.

Lack of focus is an extremely common problem—one that can have a serious impact on self-confidence. Unfocused teens often have trouble concentrating, staying on task, making decisions, and planning, and they may not have any idea why—or what to do about it. A program grad, Sara, told us that because she couldn't focus on lessons in class or remember important information, she'd come to believe she was stupid. She thought she *couldn't* learn.

Sara couldn't concentrate. Teachers would point things out to her again and again, but she couldn't remember them. Her grades in math and science were slipping.

In third grade, Sara had a teacher who loved math and science and didn't have patience with students like her who didn't share his passion. Sara tried to meet the teacher's expectations, but no matter how hard she worked, she couldn't seem to get it. The teacher chastised Sara for her poor work. She came to believe she was stupid and couldn't learn. She didn't say anything to her parents because she was ashamed and embarrassed. At the end of the year, her parents were so shocked at her low grades that they took her to a psychiatrist.

The psychiatrist diagnosed Sara with Attention Deficit Disorder, but she still believed she was just stupid. Her confidence in herself was shattered.

Sara's dad sent her to SuperCamp in the hope that it would help her regain some self-esteem. When Sara came home from camp, she was glowing. She told him she was tired of feeling stupid. It was negative thinking, not reality, that had caused her to believe it in the first place.

Sara's grades in science and math skyrocketed. Her belief in her intelligence allowed her to overcome the obstacles that kept her from learning. Today she's unstoppable!

Teens are just as mystified by their lack of focus as their parents may be. They would focus if they could. But particularly when they get bored, they don't know how to keep their minds on what they're doing.

After years of listening and working with this problem, we've found that teens stay in focus by shifting their attitudes and applying a few basic concentration skills. When they develop the skill of keeping themselves in a focused, interested, learning state, they learn more. It seems obvious, and yet it's easily overlooked.

Here's Your Moment!

Tuning out is usually the first symptom of boredom. When people start zoning out, they need to be able to shift back to the present—

they need to remind themselves that This Is It! Time to get moving, ditch the comfort zone, and jump into whatever's going down!

Campers can train themselves to monitor their states and move back into the moment whenever they feel themselves slipping. Boredom only happens in the Comfort Zone. Excitement, challenge, and growth happen in the Learning Zone. When you're in the Learning Zone, *you can't be bored!*

One of the things that keeps the Learning Zone from becoming safe and boring is that it's constantly expanding. The more you explore its boundaries, the more they stretch. That's why learning requires them to go after bigger and bigger challenges. There's no staying the same in the Learning Zone. You're either growing or you're slipping back into safety.

Boost Your Concentration: Load Up on WIIFMs

Once we had a camper, Katie, who came to us very unfocused. Throughout the early parts of the program she kept thinking about giving up and going home. We tried to help by giving her whatever tasks would distract her from the urge to quit. On day nine, during a simulation for practicing new skills in real life, three team leaders were trying to distract her, offering her fun things to do. She stayed strong and told them, "I need to focus. I want to graduate SuperCamp."

Katie got focused when she got in touch with her WIIFMs.

WIIFM stands for What's In It For Me? It's the motivating force behind nearly everything we do. Teens and adults alike can accomplish almost anything when their WIIFMs are strong enough. The most powerful WIIFMs are immediate—pleasure we'll gain right away, rather than at some undetermined future time. They're also positive. We're more likely to motivate ourselves to gain pleasure than we are to avoid pain.

Let's say a teen has just been given the task of memorizing all fifty U.S. state capitals for a test next week. What's the thought that's going through her head? The same thought that goes through anyone's mind when they face a new task: "What's in it for me?" We may not be consciously aware of asking this, but the question's there.

For most young people, the only clear answer to that question in a situation like this one is "a passing grade on the geography test." How motivating is that? As adults, we feel a strong temptation to add something like, "It's for your future. How well you do on this task today will make an impact on your college career." The adult who says this is right, but the teen may have difficulty getting in touch with the idea.

Teens aren't likely to focus a lot on learning those fifty capitals if the only motivation she's got is "It will help me—some day." But when their WIIFMs are strong enough, they pay attention.

Intrinsic motivation, which by definition comes from within, is the most powerful motivator. Nobody can motivate kids just by telling them to be more motivated. Instead, we help teens tap into the powerful WIIFMs that are *already built into* school success—WIIFMs they might not have realized were there—like the great feeling of learning something new and the thrill of accomplishment.

We do this by tapping into successes they've had already—and every teen has had some. We help them relive previous successes, then we ask them, "How did it feel?" They glow with the memory. Success feels *great*. It's an emotional rush. We help them celebrate those moments and tap into their power. They learn to build new successes on previous ones. The spark gets brighter and brighter. Once they get a taste for what it feels like to succeed, they're hooked! The rush of success becomes an increasingly powerful WIIFM—strong enough to motivate them to sit up, pay attention, and jump into their schoolwork with full concentration.

The hunger for success is a powerful WIIFM, but we can add more. The more WIIFMs an experience carries, the greater the effort we give it. When teens focus more on what turns them on about school, they become more deeply engaged in it. Concentrating on the things they do enjoy, and making choices that give them more chances to experience those things, make the WIIFMs stronger: "I love basketball. My school's team requires a minimum 3.5 GPA to participate. A higher GPA means I can get on the team."

Then there are the other less tangible WIIFMs that can add to the whole package such as easier study sessions and finishing math and reading assignments in about half the time. Oh yes, and our personal favorite: more *fun!*

Catch Those Alpha Waves and Ride

Ever seen an NBA basketball star standing at the free-throw line? What's going on behind the basket? Fans are jostling and yelling; camera flashes are popping. How do they focus with all that commotion?

They know how to get into a mental state that locks out the chaos.

Teens are hardly ever taught how to get into alpha state, which is where concentration comes naturally. The alpha state of brain activity has been closely researched and documented for decades, but most of the general public still isn't aware of its effect on learning. In this state, we read twice as fast and comprehend far more. We stay naturally alert and focused. When teens learn how to get themselves into alpha state, they're able to concentrate better and retain more.

We've all been in the alpha state, whether we were conscious of it at the time or not. Imagine you're sitting in your living room watching a really great movie. Somebody comes into the room to ask if you want more popcorn and you jump out of your chair. You were so engrossed in the movie, you forgot about your surroundings. You were in alpha state.

In less than a minute, teens can learn the five steps to get themselves into alpha state whenever they need to be there. They can put themselves into it with a simple exercise: Sit up. Take a deep breath. Close your eyes. Think of a peaceful place—a park, a beach, a lake, your yard, wherever you're most relaxed and alert—even if it's an imaginary place. With that peaceful place in mind and your eyes still closed, let your eyes look up into your head. Then look down and open your eyes.

After a couple of practices, teens can put themselves into alpha state whenever they need to. When they find themselves wandering out of alpha, they can repeat these five steps and put themselves back into it.

For many, the idea of taking charge of their own state of mind comes as a surprise. It never occurred to them that they could control the state they're in. "State," as we define it, is like a snapshot of a mood or emotion. It has three parts: thought, feeling, and body. The thought is connected to the feeling; the feeling is expressed through body posture.

It does take practice to get into the habit of "state management," but the process isn't complicated. It's mostly a matter of teaching ourselves to recognize what particular states look and feel like—and reminding ourselves that we're the ones choosing them. For instance, in our programs, we start with two teams and four flashcards. The cards read: *excited, frustrated, interested,* and *disappointed.* We select volunteers to pick a card and act out the state. Teens take turns identifying different states from the volunteers' postures.

Then comes the big question, "Who controls your state? Right now, slouch down, slow your breathing, and say to yourself, 'this is boring.' Feel uninterested in what's happening. You just put yourself in a state called Boredom. Now sit up. Breathe from the top of your chest. Move your eyes up and look straight ahead. Say to yourself, 'This is fascinating!' The state you're experiencing now is called Interest. Notice what happened? Who made it happen?"

The light bulbs go on in their heads: We have the ability to change our state whenever we want to! No matter what the circumstance, *we are each in control of our state.*

What matters most about state is that it impacts results. State and results are linked. A state of boredom in class affects concentration, which affects how much you learn. Keeping yourself in a state of interest automatically keeps you more focused, which makes you learn more.

Act As If

So what do we do if we don't like the state we're in? How do we shift it? Everyone in the room knows how to do this—they just don't *know* they know. We ask them, "How many of you have ever faked an emotion in front of your friends or parents? Acted in a way you didn't feel at the moment because you had something to gain from acting and feeling in a different way?"

They can relate. They've acted super-mature and responsible when they're trying to convince Dad to let them take the car for the weekend. Or when they've done something wrong and they think it will make the consequences less severe, they know how to play remorseful. This is nothing against teens—don't we adults do this sometimes too?

But isn't it weird how convincing we can be? We even start to convince ourselves. Act As If, and sure enough, you start to feel it!

Pretend you're sitting in skydiving class, learning to open your parachute. Right after the lecture, you've got to be ready to jump. How are you sitting? You're in a state of focused eager attention! By Acting As If, you've gotten yourself into a prime state to learn whatever lesson comes next.

A teen who's bored in history class, for instance, can improve her concentration by pretending the lesson is the most fascinating thing she's ever heard. She can hang on every word and ask her teacher to go into more detail on key points. The net result: she learns almost as much from assuming a state of interest as she would if she actually were a history buff.

And whenever that little negative voice pops into their heads— "Don't do that. You might look stupid. What will everyone think?"—they can "Jam It" before it pulls them out of state. By jamming the voice with another thought, they can keep themselves in the state they want. Anyone who starts to slip back into a negative pattern, thinking, "I'll never get this kind of math problem," can quickly re-engage by jamming it down with, "Unless I give it all I've got, so here I go!" It does take some practice, but with effort, the skill of state management gets stronger with time.

Change One—Change All Three

"How many of you have gotten into a heated argument with somebody—to the point where you were so upset you started saying things you really didn't mean?"

Everybody identifies with this. We've all been there.

"Assuming you didn't start fighting physically, what usually happens?"

Usually, one or both people walk away.

"And what happens when you walk away?"

Usually everyone calms down.

That's it. Our states have three parts: thoughts, feelings, and body posture. When we walked away—when we changed what our bodies were doing—our emotions started to cool and we began to think about the things we should have said. A change in body posture changed the feeling, which in turn changed the thought. Change one, change all three.

SLANT: Five Easy Ways to Improve Focus

Teens who regularly SLANT in class automatically get results. (SLANT strategy adapted from Dr. Ed Ellis) SLANTing alone can score better grades on report cards. Here's how to SLANT: Sit up, Lean forward, Ask questions, Nod your head, and Talk to the teacher. SLANTing works because it keeps the student more engaged and focused—and actually helps the teacher teach better. Campers

Not long ago, science assumed the human brain didn't change much beyond childhood. We now know that our brains change constantly. Our experiences, thoughts, feelings, and actions affect the wiring of our brains.

In modern times, when we're all living hectic, information-saturated lives, our brains are changing faster than ever before. Teens' brains today are different than teens' brains ten years ago. To reach these new turbo-charged brains effectively, our teaching methods need to change with the times.

Quantum Learning methods—the ones that form SuperCamp's programs—are about matching the way we give information to the way teens think: getting in teens' worlds. That matching is what keeps our methods evolving dynamically and keeps us relevant year after year.

are amazed when they discover they can actually influence how well their teachers teach. We do a skit in which a teen tells us about a recent trip he took while the facilitator looks away, twirls her hair, slouches, and says nothing. Then we ask the teen to repeat the story. This time, the facilitator sits up, nods enthusiastically, and asks questions. Then we ask, "What did you notice this second time about how the story was told?"

They all notice that the second time the story was told a lot better. Why? Because the teller had a better audience!

Sitting up keeps our bodies more alert. Leaning forward is a cue to our minds and feelings that we're interested. Nodding signals to us and our listeners that we are following what's being said. And talking to the teacher and asking questions turns a one-way monologue into a dynamic interaction.

Here's the Big Picture—Where Are You?

We've seen how teens can help themselves stay focused by adjusting their attitudes and states and by applying a few basic concentration skills. They can also maintain a laser-like focus by staying aware of the big picture—and their place in it.

With practice, teens can learn to view each day in terms of the big picture. They can develop the habit of positioning themselves in that picture as the masterminds behind their self-creation. It's difficult to be bored when you're in control; it's even more difficult *when you believe what you're doing matters.*

CHAPTER 7

Turning Low Motivation into Goal Achievement

Scott showed some extraordinary abilities at an early age: a phenomenal memory and a passion for airplanes. But because he was a little slower getting started with his reading, his teachers had him tested for a learning disability. The tests came back negative, but the seed of self-doubt had been planted in Scott's mind. Scott's parents could see that he was holding himself back.

In fifth grade, Scott's reading and other scores qualified him for the Duke University gifted program, but he still failed to make the list of high achievers at his school. One day, the high achievers were pulled out of class to attend a leadership conference. Scott was one of four runners-up who failed to make the cut. When he got in the car at the end of the day, he looked down at the floor and said, "Everyone else got to go on a field trip, but I was too dumb to go."

With that lack of belief in himself, how would Scott be motivated to challenge himself, to grow into his own considerable abilities?

"How many of you have ever ridden a bike?"

The group is full of quizzical faces. Everybody's ridden a bicycle but they're not clear yet where we're going with this. *How's a bicycle wheel going to help me learn?*

"What's a bicycle do for you?" the facilitator asks. "It lets you do more with less. It's designed to give the rider maximum distance for minimal work. A high-performance bike is a system designed to give a high level of performance for the effort the rider puts in. Wouldn't it be cool to have a system like that for schoolwork? Or for just about anything else you decided to go after? A way to get more out of the effort you put in? Let's ask Curtis here to help us with this demonstration. Now, Curtis is a cyclist. He's got a 1972 Schwinn Flyer. Banana seat, front and rear fenders, little streamers coming off the ends of the handlebars..."

Some of the campers are snickering.

"What? Curtis is a serious cyclist! So maybe he doesn't have a high-caliber racing machine but he tries really hard. Last year I invited Curtis to compete in the annual charity bike race. He shows up with his Schwinn and the first thing he notices is that all the other bicycles don't look like his bicycle. They're all the latest equipment: high-tech alloys, ergonomic designs, twenty-one speeds, all set to the correct ratios. At first, Curtis is discouraged. Then he gets this crazy idea: He decides he's going to win the race anyway! He's going to put so much energy and effort into this race that he'll win. The question is: Will he win the race?"

Most of the campers are in an optimistic mood and they're rooting for Curtis, so they yell, "Yes!"

The facilitator shakes his head. "The answer is NO! There's no way he's going to win that race. We could try bribing him with a two-week extreme adventure vacation to New Zealand, all expenses paid. Anything he wants. Just win the race. Now he's thinking, 'Oh, man. I just *have* to win this race.' Will he win?"

The teens yell, "NO!"

"Well, what if we coach him? Teach him how to use his body, how to think like a racer? Then will he win?"

"NO!"

"How about we threaten him? Win the race or else. Now he'll win, right?"

"NOOO!"

"Why not? He's got a great attitude, good posture, he's motivated. Why won't he win the race?"

They understand that Curtis is doomed to lose *because the system he's using isn't powerful enough!*

A bicycle is a system we use to get around. We also use systems for learning—and for accomplishing our goals in life. Sometimes parents see their teenagers falling behind in school and life, and they blame their attitude and motivation level. They question their child's commitment. But maybe the issue isn't attitude. Maybe they don't yet have a *system* for tackling school and life. Maybe they're struggling because they're stuck on Curtis' 1972 Schwinn with its banana seat!

"Okay, let's say we pool together and buy Curtis a really primo racing bicycle. It costs $9,500. You can pick it up with your pinky. Curtis takes one look at his new bike and says, 'Cool! Now that I've got this awesome equipment, I don't even have to pedal. This bike will do all the work for me.' Will he win the race?"

The campers shout, "NO!"

"Well why not? He's got the equipment."

They get it now. Effort alone isn't enough. A powerful system isn't enough. *You have to put a great system together with effort.* Then you'll win the race!

Some young people have great equipment, but for one reason or another don't put in the effort. They may not believe in their abilities. They may not be aware of their own strengths or recognize the value in pursuing the things they're passionate about. They may be making assumptions that aren't true: "I can't talk to my teacher" or "My teacher doesn't like me." Many kids don't think they have the right to do things—like go to the teacher or request special help. Or, like some obviously gifted individuals, they may think their giftedness alone is all they need, that they don't have to put in any effort to develop their abilities.

Parents often complain that their sons and daughters aren't reaching their full potential. They know they're capable of much more, but they don't know how to motivate them to go for it. But has any human being ever reached their *full* potential? What matters is whether they're *reaching for* their potential—whether they're challenging themselves, stretching, and growing. To do that, they've got to have both the system that allows them to accomplish it, and the commitment to make the effort.

What *does* get them motivated? What really lights their fire? What does motivation look like? What *do* you do when you're motivated? Let's look at some of the reasons teenagers give for low motivation and what we can do to help them give their best effort.

Motivation: You Can't Make Me!

Motivation is the *effort* the rider puts into pedaling—or more precisely, the thing that makes the rider want to put in that effort. Parents don't need us to tell them that you can't force a teen to get motivated. It has to come from within.

Motivation is different from self-discipline. SuperCamp facilitator John Le Tellier says self-discipline is doing what needs to be done, when it needs to be done, when you *don't* want to do it. Motivation is doing what needs to be done, when it needs to be done, when you *want* to do it. Motivation has passion in it.

Motivation isn't the same thing as desire, either. Teens and adults alike can want something very badly, something that's well within their reach, but still refuse to go after it. People create barriers to the things they want. It's easier to create barriers in your head than to take action. For many people, failure is a safety blanket: "I got poor results because I didn't really try." What's sabotaging our motivation in this case is our fear of failure. Not giving something our full effort is taking the easy way out. It keeps us from looking bad and feeling foolish, but it also robs us of achieving our dreams.

We seldom think of it this way, but learning how to reframe

failure, to mine it for lessons, is an important life-skill. Failure is an unavoidable part of life. It's a necessary ingredient in success. It's how we learn what to do differently next time! The more positively we can approach our failures, the less power they'll have to sap our motivation.

When teens talk about their heroes, we like to ask them what those heroes did that was so great. It sometimes comes as a revelation to them that their heroes weren't born that way. They had to become great. They struggled, too. Lance Armstrong didn't hop right out of his hospital bed and immediately win a race. What matters is not whether heroes struggled or failed, but that they kept going.

One of the signs that campers read on our walls says, "If It's to Be, It's Up to Me." In other words, they have a responsibility to take Ownership of their dreams. With their dreams on this footing, they begin to see that they practically have an *obligation* to pursue their passions. That's when choosing to live Above the Line takes on a new meaning. Giving in to their fear of failure, whining, blaming external forces for their lack of trying—that's all Below the Line stuff, because it means their dreams get neglected.

Sometimes when people shy away from pursuing their goals it's because they don't see why their dreams matter to the rest of the world. It can come as a major "Aha!" for teens when they realize that the thing they want most isn't just a selfish fantasy but a real, wonderful contribution they can make to the world. When they begin to see that their greatest gifts to the world lie in their passions, they begin to have a stronger sense of responsibility toward their own dreams.

Live Your Dreams: The Success Model Points to Who We Are

Sara was a quiet, serious, and intensely focused girl who had trouble approaching people and making friends. Whenever she got ready to approach someone, she'd get afraid and wouldn't follow through. When she applied the Failure Leads to Success key, she started approaching people more—in spite of her fear. When she did that, she began to realize something: The people she talked to were benefiting from interacting with her! People told her she came across as trustworthy. Once she realized she had something to offer people just by being herself, she was able to approach people easily.

Sometimes, low-motivated young people are being held back by a lack of self-knowledge. They haven't yet recognized their own strengths. They don't have a clear picture of what they have to offer others. Like Sara, when they realize they have some great qualities that others enjoy and admire, their confidence level takes off.

In our programs, the Success Model gives campers small victories that they can build on. The more they experience success, the more they discover what's so great about themselves. As they're exploring their own strengths, they have an opportunity to write "I am…" and then challenge themselves to see how many times they can complete the sentence. "I am a son." "I am fast." "I am funny." And so on. Self-knowledge is a powerful confidence-builder. It's also a lens. It helps people discover the passions that can keep them motivated for a lifetime.

Purpose, Passion, Direction: Who I Am Makes a Difference

Even though it was years ago, we still love to tell the story of a girl, Erin, who was an inspiration to us and to all the other campers in the program. She showed us how much is possible when your attitude is right.

Erin came to the program in a wheelchair. She'd been in a car accident at a young age. Most of the program proved no challenge for her, but day five is Outdoor Adventure Day, when teens climb a thirty-foot pole, do trust falls, and walk aerial obstacle courses. Of course Erin was excused from these activities, so we were amazed when she wheeled over, tugged on one of our sleeves, and told us she wanted to climb the pole. We didn't want to discourage her from trying, but we couldn't imagine how she'd do it. So when she went for it, we stood nearby, supportively cheering her on.

She had little or no strength in her legs and used her arm muscles alone to reach the top of the pole. It took her a long time and a lot of effort; but she did it.

Erin became a celebrity not only to the campers but also to the facilitators and adult leaders. She was the model of commitment and determination—what a person can do if she really believes in herself. Erin *wanted* to climb the pole. She didn't let a little thing like not being able to use her legs stop her!

Our passions and dreams are the *real* motivators in our lives: the things we want deep down. When we act from these motivations, nothing stops us. We're ready to look at the obstacles that are keeping us from our goals as *things to be overcome*, rather than as barriers.

If It's to Be, It's Up to Me: Setting Extraordinary Goals

No dream ever comes true, no obstacle is ever overcome, no goal is ever reached without focused action. Yet young people are seldom specifically taught how to set and pursue goals.

They may not have a strong sense of what a goal really is. We help them see that a goal is *a plan for action*. It's about translating promising ideas into useful, acceptable applications. Or to put it in simpler terms, it's a plan to *use* your great idea.

Of course we're talking about worthwhile and realistic goals here, specifically the ones that will get teens to their stated dreams. We do help teens see that there are practical goals and those that are long shots. We help them learn to follow their dreams while being realistic and having a back-up plan.

Campers start creating their goals by formulating a specific plan of action. They analyze several possible ways to reach their goal. They consider sources of assistance and resistance. They discover that they're capable of setting goals in several arenas of their lives: personal, school, career, family, social, and others. They find that it helps to sort their goals into short, medium, and long-term. We ask them to write down the expectations they have for their goals.

We also challenge them to be clear on their purpose for going after this goal. Are you going to ace AP chemistry to get a good grade, or to make it into Stanford's chemistry program? Getting the A is a happy byproduct of doing great in class, but it's not the main objective.

Part of the challenge for parents is to find out what teens think of their own potential: "Who am I?" "Where can I see myself going in life?" "What's the most incredible life I can think of living?" At its heart, goal-setting is about knowing who you are and what you're about. The only reason for goals to exist is to help us apply ourselves to the world at large. Self-knowledge is at the bottom of it all.

The difference between the life that you have and the life that you want is merely a matter of responsible choices.

I'll Do Whatever It Takes

A boy named Johnny, who had a drive for leadership, once came into our program. He wanted to attend camp because he'd heard it taught leadership skills. Unfortunately, his parents couldn't manage the cost of tuition. Johnny found a friend who was willing to pay part of the tuition, but if he wanted to go, he'd have to raise the rest himself. Johnny made a commitment; he was going to get himself to camp. He spent the next two weeks calling people and asking them to pledge $10 or $20 toward his program tuition. A lot of people said no—they couldn't see the benefit in it. But Johnny kept working at it. Just days before the program began, Johnny made the full cost of tuition.

By the time he came into the program, Johnny had already developed a great sense of his own ability to make things happen: "It means a lot that I can influence people and set an example that others can follow." By the time he reached us, Johnny already knew a lot about doing whatever it took to achieve a goal. He was an inspiration to facilitators and campers alike because *he found a way to reach his goal.*

One of the most powerful Keys of Excellence is the Commitment key. Something incredible happens when we commit to something. We lock ourselves into a course of action. Once we make a commitment, we discover all kinds of resources we didn't know were available. It's powerful stuff.

Making a commitment to achieve a goal, no matter what it takes, means people have to become the masters of their own internal dialogue. This one's a toughie even for adults because we're often not even conscious of the things we say to ourselves. Often, we've gotten so accustomed to telling ourselves certain things that we're barely aware we're doing it. But our brains believe the things we tell them, so when we're trying to replace old behaviors with new ones, we have to be ready to counter those old messages.

Just as negative habits can limit a person's ability to overcome challenges, positive habits can expand them. Many have found that they can flip their negative self-talk by adding "up until now" to a negative phrase whenever it accidentally pops out. If they find themselves saying, "I stink at math," they can quickly add, "—up until now." They find that this phrase forces the past back where it belongs: in the past. In other words: "I can't do it—YET! But I will soon!"

Some teens have found that when a negative thought creeps up they can Jam It with a positive one. They can replace "I'll never run a mile in five minutes" with "I know I can do this."

When they feel themselves giving in to fears and doubts, they sometimes find it helpful to do a *redirect*. Instead of giving any more thought to the negatives, they can focus all their thoughts and energies on the very next step toward their goal. It's all about action. Instead of wasting time internally, they can focus on doing whatever it takes to grab that next rung on the ladder.

Breaking Through: If I Can Do This, I Can Do Anything

"What you're about to experience combines everything we've learned in this program. It involves having a specific vision and goals for your life, and then getting into the most resourceful state to get to that goal. It involves truly tapping into the greatness within you and believing in yourself."

Something special's going down; we can all feel it. The music is proud, strong, full of power. We pass around 12-by-12-inch pine boards and markers.

"This activity is *not* about breaking a piece of wood. It's a metaphor about life. It's about how you can get what you want in your life. It's about breaking barriers to grab on to your goals. Today is about *going for it* no matter what."

They have the power to break through any barrier. It has nothing to do with body size or physical condition. The skinniest, smallest teens will break through the board almost as easily as the hulking, muscular ones.

Campers can't just walk in off the street and accomplish this. That's why we put it close to the end of the session. By now they have a much higher level of confidence and focus than they had before they arrived. We do a lot to prepare them for this moment. They have a lot of support and coaching. We're at the absolute top of our game for this exercise: clear, focused, enthusiastic, in state.

We talk to them about the reasons they might have had for not reaching their goals in the past. Maybe they got lazy and decided it wasn't worth the effort. Maybe they failed and let their fear of failure hold them back. But this exercise is about putting the past where it belongs. Today is about making new choices.

By this point in the program, they've all chosen a goal to pursue. We ask them to think of the goal they've set for themselves. We ask them to envision achieving that goal, to make it a reality. Then they write their goals on the boards.

When they're finished, we ask them to flip the boards over. "Where is your goal?"

"Under the board."

"This board is the obstacle that has come between you and your dreams. What is it that's holding you back from what you really want? Get honest. Get real. What barrier, what fear has ripped you off over and over again?"

When they have their answers, they pick up their pens and write their obstacles on the board—on the opposite side from their goal. An inch of pine now stands between them and their dreams.

Now it's time to get in state. They're expert state-managers by this point, so when we tell them to get into a state of focused excitement, the energy builds at once. Powerful music swells loudly. They get into a powerful physical stance and repeat, "I am centered, focused, confident, and powerful."

"Be ready for success. It's yours…if you choose it."

When they can *feel* their commitment, they're ready.

The facilitators and their teammates gather around. The support is strong. One by one, they break through the barriers and grab their goals!

All around us teens are laughing, crying, hugging, and holding up the broken pieces of their boards. The confidence radiating from their faces is beautiful.

We remember a camper who had a gorgeous voice but, because of her insecurity, would only sing in the shower. She wrote her fear of being heard on her board and broke through it. When she told us this during the final night of sharing, campers began chanting, "Do it now! You can do it!" With the energy building, she got up in front of the entire group and belted out a song. Everybody was crying.

Teens have told us that when they're really ready to break through to their goals, it's almost as if the board parts for them. There's no resistance. Their hands go right through. One person told us, "In the one moment I broke through my board, I put all my focus and intention into it. And I realized, if I can do this, I can do anything."

This exercise is unequivocal. You can't argue with your ability to succeed when you're holding those two pieces of broken board in your hands.

Imagine if your child had that level of confidence.

CONCLUSION

Using What Works
for Your Teen's Success

This book has been all about the breakthroughs that help teens turn problems into strengths. Throughout these pages you've gotten a peek through the keyhole at the way we facilitate these moments. The processes we use to help teens arrive at these shifts are particular to our program, but the principles behind them are universal and timeless. Within a supportive environment, breakthroughs can happen at any moment. Get ready to experience the shift in your teen!

It's the last day of the program. As moms and dads arrive to pick up their sons and daughters, anticipation hangs in the air. If you could imagine little cartoon bubbles over the parents' heads, they'd say things like: "I wonder if I'll notice a difference. How long will it take for the effects of this program to show up? Has she forgiven me for making her go?"

The parents are seated in a large room. One of the facilitators talks with them for a while about what to expect. Teens usually go in one of two directions when they're reunited with their parents. They're either bubbling with excitement, talking a mile a minute, trying to tell the whole of what they've learned in a flurry of words. Or they're silent. Pensive. Unsure how to move back into the old grooves of their lives after so much has changed. They feel a need to internalize what they experienced for a while before talking about it.

Facilitators tell parents, "During the past ten days, everything they know has been taken apart and reassembled."

That's how it happens in our programs. But it doesn't have to happen all at once during ten intense days. Many teens write us that the real magic happens, not during the program, but weeks or months later in the course of day-to-day living. Every day brings opportunities for defining moments—times when they have a chance to shift the course of their lives.

Parent Heidi Fuller wrote, "My words can't do justice to the words my son spoke after arriving home from SuperCamp, words he would have been too fearful and self-conscious to use before. Simple words like hug, friendship, closeness. He told us he made hugging friends. Then he hugged me. And he made me be the one to let go first. Then I caught sight of his fingernails. He'd allowed some of the girls to color them with Sharpee pens at SuperCamp. He ran downstairs and put on his "no FIMAGE" T-shirt and came back up to show us he was not afraid of the choice he had made to let go of his fear of image. The best way to wrap it all up is to say that this boy who was calling it "StupidCamp" (thinking it was for his learning disability and being pretty down on it before he arrived there) has now asked if he can go back next year and hopes that some of the friends he made this year will return with him. It's hard to express what this hope and optimism feel like after so many years of struggle and worry."

What teens discover in our programs is supposed to be taken home. It's intended for them to keep it going once they leave us and adapt it to their day-to-day life. Teens, parents, and teachers write to us about ways they've made the processes they learned in our programs work for them at home and at school. After all, it's what they do to affect the world *outside* camp that matters.

Most teens come to us with one or more of the seven problems we've discussed in this book. When they leave at the end of ten days, the problem is still there, but what's changed is the way they orient *themselves* to these challenges. Labeling is still labeling, but they've discovered how much larger they are than any label. Their school workload is just as heavy, but they can now tackle it with joy, confidence, purpose—and some dynamite study habits. Their absentee parent is still absent, but they have let go of the resentment that was poisoning all their other relationships.

What is there for a parent to do? While teens are shifting their orientation to the world, parents can facilitate the change by *shifting their orientation to their teens*. Nobody can keep doing things the same way and expect to get different results. We know that all families have learned a dance. It's not often optimal, but everyone knows the steps. When one of the partners changes steps, it usually means that the other partners need to make corresponding changes or they may all fall back into the original dance.

Parents of SuperCamp graduates want to make that change stick. We have follow-up resources, products, and even Parent Weekends to support this desire, and many parents take cues directly from their teens. When parents change the way they interact with their sons and daughters, they pave the way for transformation.

With these thoughts in mind, let's take a last look at the seven greatest challenges teens face, and how they can turn them into strengths.

Bridges Rebuilt: Troubled Relationships Can Heal

We love hearing from teens and parents who have found ways to reconnect. We always trust that the loving bond is still there no matter what might have happened to damage it or drive it into hiding. With courage and love, young people and their parents can reconnect and rebuild their relationships.

Remember Andy from Chapter 1, who acted as though his mom owed him the use of her car? When Andy began to develop the ability to step out of himself and into other people's worlds, his attitude started to shift. He told his mom that learning about other people's lives made him realize he needed to show more appreciation for things. He retrained himself to ask for the car and explain why he needed it. If his mom said no, he accepted her answer. No demands. No raised voice. No attitude.

What made the difference for Andy and his mom? We could boil it down to a shift in perspective: seeing things from another person's point of view. When teens and parents really work at understanding one another, they create a bond of trust. They know they will be heard, that their point of view will be respected, not judged, ridiculed, or condemned. Just the act of respecting another person's point of view strengthens a relationship.

Parents also discovered that things got better between themselves and their teens when they learned to respect their teenagers' privacy. Teens are just beginning to recognize that they're separate entities from their parents; for them, the separation is fragile. They have a great need for privacy. They want adults to treat their spaces and possessions with the same respect they'd show a grown-up's.

Many parents found that their kids' lives got back on the right track as soon as they started making more time for them. Teens know whether or not they're a priority to their parents. It's tough for a young person to feel bad about himself or resentful of a parent when the parent puts him first.

It helps to have something of common interest to talk about—upcoming events or activities—to keep the lines of communication open even when things get tense. Parents who share sports, hobbies, or other activities with their sons and daughters have a built-in point of contact.

Connection and mutual respect: these are the primary materials in building bridges between adults and teens. Basic communication techniques like the Four-Part Apology and Open the Front Door facilitate the process.

Too Big for Labels, Too Real for Rejection: How Teens Overcome Emotional Hurt

Young people who have a deep-down sense of themselves are a lot less likely to be tripped up by failures, labels, and rejections. When they know themselves, it's tough to get a label to stick on them. And if they also approach failure as an opportunity to gather information for their next try, they won't get derailed when the results don't turn out the way they planned.

What keeps the self-discovery process going after teens have left camp is a steady stream of positive experiences: being known and liked for who they are, putting their identities and passions into action, and giving the world a chance to see "the real me." Parents who encourage and support their children's interests—and who themselves demonstrate a positive attitude toward failure—can help them become strong enough to weather rejections and setbacks. The dance in the family changes when a teen comes home with new skills and behaviors. Parents can end up learning great skills from their teens such as new ways of communicating, apologizing, and making their wants known. They have an opportunity to adopt new ways of interacting and thinking.

It's about supporting their belief that they have something wonderful to offer just as they are. Ashley, who retreated into books when somebody told her that her laugh was stupid, learned that just being herself was cool. She still loves reading, but now she schedules it around her many social engagements. Lots of people want to share a laugh with her!

Unstoppable! Turning Around Negative Self-Image

Young people with negative self-images really blossom when they and their parents keep a relentless focus on the positive—when they acknowledge every effort and celebrate every achievement. It's not just about praising them for what they've done but also for who they are.

It snowballs over time: success builds on success. After a while they reach a tipping point. Negative self-image falls away and the unstoppable dynamo within them surges ahead. Once they acquire a taste for success, once they see how much they're *really* capable of doing, there's no stopping them. Maddie, whose teacher told her she was dumb, decided she wanted to be the kind of person who was inspired to do great things. Her little bit of shyness and reservation disappeared, and were replaced by self-confidence and self-assuredness. The girl who was once told she was too stupid to be in the gifted English class went on to ace AP English along with AP Calculus and Physics—and also won four consecutive awards for community service.

Duncan, the boy who was ostracized because he marched to a different drummer, and was always inventing things and asking questions, decided to embrace the things that made him different. He would not let social conventions hold him back from having a great life. He embarked on pathways few have traveled and is today finishing a triple major at Tufts University.

Program grad Nehemiah Green wrote us of how it felt when he turned his self-image around, "Now when I speak to people I'm no longer afraid to look into their eyes."

It makes our day to see a previously shy teen stand up tall and face the world with confidence. The confidence is theirs to discover; no one can hand it to them. But parents can make sure that the evidence of their sons' and daughters' greatness is all around them—that it's recognized and acknowledged.

I've Still Got Me: How Teens Rise Above Disruptive Change

Parents are sometimes surprised to find their kids are doing okay despite massive changes or tragic circumstances. Program grad Brett Higdon told us, "The mind is a very powerful thing and can overcome anything."

Parents have told us that the best thing they can do to help them overcome difficult times is simply to listen—with an ear to finding out what they need. Are there questions they need answered? Do they simply need a little space to work through it on their own? When young people feel that they're really being heard, their point of view is respected, and their needs matter, they're less likely to be overwhelmed by disruptive events.

We know that teens have a reputation for being emotionally sensitive. But what we see in them is a reservoir of strength. We've seen time and again that they're able to recognize that no matter what has happened, they're still themselves—nothing can take that away. When people have a strong sense of who they are, they're better prepared to stand up to life changes and challenges.

Create a Learning Space: How to Put the Muscle in Weak Academic Performance

Teens launch out of our programs with a burning passion for learning. Parents write enthusiastically about ways they've helped keep that excitement going at home. Parents who intentionally create a learning environment in their homes find that their sons and daughters are better able to develop the study skills they learned in our programs. Mastering these skills gives them a confidence boost. Program grad Grayson Hurd wrote, "In some ways, high school, because of my tools and skills, has been easier for me than middle school was."

We've found that it helps a lot for them to have their own personalized study space, an area adapted to the way they as individuals learn best: low or bright light, absolute quiet or background noise. Grads also report that it helps a lot to establish regular study times.

Aside from skills and space, it's about keeping the focus on the fun. "I see Peter liking school," Dr. J. Kolb said of his son's newfound confidence. "Peter stands taller now!" Learning is an adventure. Teens who stay in this mindset do better and reach further. Remember Cody, the student whose parents thought he might one day claw his way up to a C average? His mom wrote us, "I just got Cody's report card...he made Honor Roll!"

Laser-Focus: No Room for Poor Concentration
When Passion's in the Picture

Parents often get frustrated over their sons' and daughters' lack of concentration because they don't know what to do about it. They often fall back on blaming their kids. A lot of factors can influence teens' ability to concentrate, but for most it comes down to a lack of focusing skills and just plain boredom. Parents who encourage their teens' passions often find that their lack of focus is self-correcting.

Sometimes, when they start chasing their passions, even those things they once saw as faults become strengths. David, who had trouble focusing, told us what he learned about the Attention Deficit Disorder that used to hold him back: "One characteristic of ADD is that if you're not interested in something you can't focus on it, even with medication. But if you are interested, you hyper-focus on it. I found myself forgetting to take my meds...I had found my passion and what I wanted to do in life. Once I was able to focus on courses in that specialty, I was able to use my ADD and my passion as my focusing tool. Ultimately, I went completely off meds...I love my work and am truly fascinated by it."

Let's See How Far I Can Go:
Helping Teens Reach for Their Potential

Nobody is bored when they're challenging themselves to bring out the greatness within. When people get enough of a taste of success, they get hooked. They develop a thirst to do more, push the envelope, and raise the bar. Many parents write that their sons' and daughters' underachievement began to turn around when *they* started to turn around the way they looked at their teens. Focusing on failures, low grades, lack of effort, and the problem, only seemed to make things worse. When parents shifted instead to the successes, talents, and victories, teens began to wake up to their own potential.

"I can achieve any goal I have," wrote Janell Wilburn. "I feel prepared to accept and meet challenges in life rather than giving up—or worse, not even trying. I realize if I'm willing to face my fears I will have the confidence to succeed in life with whatever I do."

Things I Learned from SuperCamp That Made Me a Better Foster Parent:

- Using positive language and concise directions.
  ("Remember to take your jacket.")

- Picking my battles. (Messy rooms and haircuts are NOT worthy battles)

- Knowing my teens—their music, idols, clothing, and so forth.
  (Using SuperCamp's prime directive: theirs to ours and ours to theirs)

- Not asking them too many questions—teens hate that.

- Giving them choices—"Would you like waffles or cereal for breakfast?"
  —rather than "What do you want for breakfast?"

- Making sure they know: "I'll always be here for you. I will not give up on you."

- Letting them know when they've hurt my feelings.

- Making cute posters and putting notes in their binders to remind them they're LOVED and APPRECIATED.

- Having a sense of humor and sharing inside jokes.

- Being silly, playful, and crazy—it creates amazing bonds.

- Not putting them on the spot: "Franky, tell Mrs. Smith about your new job at the bank."

- Modeling memory and academic strategies by using them myself so that my teens notice that I really use and believe in this stuff.

—Sue Sinclair Pepe

Defining Moments: How Teens Build Bridges to Greatness

Now we're down to the last few minutes of the program. The parents have been prepped for the reunion with their sons and daughters. They've been told what to expect but they're still on pins and needles. A door opens and the campers file in holding hands. One by one, parents catch sight of their son or daughter. There's a moment when their breaths catch in their throats. Then the tears begin to come.

After our graduation and concluding ceremonies, most of the teens go to their parents and embrace them. Some of these parents have not been hugged by their child in years. Something big has happened. The teens hold their heads high. They look everyone— even their parents—in the eye and speak with confidence and power. The walls are down. The masks are off. And what's more evident than anything is—love.

During the next few minutes, days, and weeks, they'll tell their families all about how they got to know an extraordinary person: themselves. And they'll explain, each in their own way, that they're thankful for their parents' support.

We hear it a lot, in one-on-one conversation and on the stage during sharing time. Even those who were resistant to attend are now glad they did. "I pleaded with my parents: 'Please don't send me!' Now I want to say thank you, Mom and Dad, for sending me here. I never knew I had so much potential."

The bridge between teens and their own excellence is built of defining moments; events that allow them to see themselves clearly in relation to the rest of the world. Our programs are successful because we deliberately create these moments. But defining moments occur naturally and spontaneously in every person's life. They can happen at any time, in any situation, to anyone. What matters is whether a person chooses to grab the gifts these moments have to offer.

It's tough for parents to recognize that there is only so much they can do to influence their sons' and daughters' greatness. During all those pre-teen years when their children were small, parents could simply do for their sons and daughters whatever needed to be done.

But now that their children are looking adulthood in the eye, the time to do for them is past. Parents have to learn how to resist the urge to do for their teens, and must stand back lovingly and supportively while they learn to *do for themselves.*

We can't hand them defining moments. But we can encourage them to go for the experiences where these moments happen. And we can listen attentively when they tell us what those moments are like for them.

A program grad, Laci, wrote us, "I find myself a happier person living a more fulfilling life." This is what we want for all young people. We believe every person has the potential for greatness, the ability to live an extraordinary life and make a unique contribution to the world. But we can't force greatness on anyone. Teens must choose for themselves whether to bring out the greatness within. Ultimately, all parents, teachers, and facilitators can do is believe in them, listen carefully, and watch in awe as they take on the world.

How to Contact SuperCamp and Quantum Learning Network

By Phone: (760) 722-0072
By Mail: Quantum Learning Network
      1938 Avenida del Oro
      Oceanside, CA 92056
Online: www.QLN.com

International associate offices in Taiwan, China, Hong Kong, South Korea, Malaysia, Singapore, Indonesia, Mexico, Dominican Republic, and Switzerland

---

Receive a Complimentary Handbook: *The 7 Biggest Teen Problems and How To Turn Them Into Strengths Handbook*
Go to: www.TeenStrengths.com

More Books by Bobbi DePorter

Quantum Success: 8 Key Catalysts to Shift Your Energy into Dynamic Focus
Quantum Business: Achieving Success Through Quantum Learning
Quantum Teaching: Orchestrating Student Success
Quantum Learning: Unleashing the Genius in You
The 8 Keys of Excellence: Principles to Live By
The Quantum Upgrade Series—
    Quantum Learner
    Quantum Reader
    Quantum Writer
    Quantum Memorizer
    Quantum Thinker
    Quantum Note-Taker

To order go to www.QLN.com